Grace

The cruciform love of God

Forthcoming in the FAITH GOING DEEPER series

Goodness   Richard Major
Faith and Unbelief   Stephen Bullivant
Sacrament   Peter Waddell

FAITH GOING DEEPER

Grace

The cruciform love of God

Peter Groves

Series editor:

Andrew Davison

CANTERBURY
PRESS

Norwich

© Peter Groves 2012

Published in 2012 by Canterbury Press
Editorial office
Invicta House, 108–114 Golden Lane,
London EC1Y 0TG

Canterbury Press is an imprint of Hymns Ancient &
Modern Ltd (a registered charity)
13a Hellesdon Park Road
Norwich NR6 5DR, UK

www.canterburypress.co.uk

British Library Cataloguing in Publication data

A catalogue record for this book is available
from the British Library

978 1 84825 054 3

Typeset by The Manila Typesetting Company
Printed and bound by
CPI Group (UK) Ltd, Croydon CR0 4YY

Contents

Introduction by the FAITH GOING DEEPER series editor

Academic theology is in good heart in these early years of the twenty-first century: much Christian thinking is confident and vigorous; there is more enthusiasm for theology among the clergy than for some decades. All the same, the work that theologians produce is not always accessible to those who should be its principal beneficiaries: the people of the Church.

With this series, *Faith Going Deeper*, the aim is to provide a bridge for Christians of all traditions to some of what is most valuable and significant in contemporary theological thinking and writing. In doing so, the series will also introduce some younger theologians to a wider, popular audience. The books deal with central themes of Christian thought and life, starting with grace, virtue, faith, and the sacraments. Their authors aim to be clear without being simplistic, and to avoid technical terms while providing a framework for understanding the subject in hand. They are assured in the truth of the Christian faith, and on that basis unafraid to face the challenges of our times.

The writers of these books, and I as the editor of the series, agree with the point Dorothy L. Sayers never tired of making, that nothing rejuvenates the mission of the Church like contact with good Christian theology. Our faith is far from dull; as Sayers put it, 'it is the neglect of dogma that makes for dullness'. With these books we hope to present again what she called 'the Divine Drama', so that it might once again 'startle the world'. That will only happen if it first of all startles the Church once again.

Andrew Davison

Cambridge

Eastertide 2012

For Beatrice, grace personified.

Acknowledgements

I am very grateful to Andrew Davison for inviting me to undertake the project, and for his perceptive editing and generous support, and to Christine Smith, Hannah Ward and Canterbury Press for similar help and expertise. Thanks are also due to those who took the time to read sections of this book or offer advice as to its contents, in particular Sarah Apetrei, Mark Edwards, Terry Irwin, Philip Endean, Simon Cuff and Tom Carpenter. I have also benefited from the support and insight of many friends, colleagues and teachers, among them Brian Davies, John Muddiman, Rowan Williams, Simon Oliver, Susan Gillingham, Simon Jones, Paul Joyce, Philip Kennedy and Diarmaid MacCulloch. Mention should also be made of the congregation of St Mary Magdalen's Oxford, forced to hear my ideas before they are fully formed, and of Martin Williams, E. J. Milner-Gulland, Timothy Knapman, Llewelyn Morgan, Ed Bispham and Anne Davies, Peter and Jane McLeod, Owen Law and Cathy Groves, and of course Beatrice, Michael and Edward.

1

What is grace?

Initiative and invitation

Towards the end of the Gospel of Luke, not long before Jesus' entry into Jerusalem and the events of his suffering and death, the evangelist tells the story of a man named Zacchaeus. It is a beautifully vivid story, beloved of children, teachers and songwriters alike, about a man so small in stature that he needed to climb a tree simply to see the arrival of the Galilean preacher about whom everybody has heard so much. For Zacchaeus, the tree is a refuge as well as a vantage point, because he is a chief tax collector. He was an important member of the hated monetary servants of the Roman authorities who harvested that which was commanded by the state, and in so doing inherited a system of profiteering and power which was relentlessly abused in the ancient world. To be a member of the crowd might, for Zacchaeus, have been an experience uncomfortable for more than visual reasons: not only is he small, he is unpopular. So he is glad that the sycamore tree is there to be climbed, and up he goes, having run on ahead to make sure he is well positioned when Jesus passes by. But Jesus does not pass him by. Instead he looks up and addresses the little observer. 'Zacchaeus, hurry and come down; for I must stay at your house today' (Luke 19.5). Zacchaeus is overjoyed, and dashes down to welcome Jesus.

Those who witness this scene are less than impressed. Why should a travelling celebrity take an interest in this dreadful man? Perhaps he does not know who he really is, though the use of his name will have confused them. Surely it is not appropriate for a godly man, a holy teacher, to be the guest of one who is a sinner? But Zacchaeus, it seems, is a man transformed. He stands before them all and announces to Jesus his new-found generosity: he will give half of his possessions to the poor, and will recompense anyone whom he has defrauded four times over.

Jesus responds to Zacchaeus' words with a telling phrase: 'Today salvation has come to this house' (Luke 19.9). As so often in the narratives of the Gospels, there is a deliberate dramatic irony at work. Salvation has come to this house, in that Zacchaeus has been changed, he has been saved from his former self, and his victims have been delivered from his financial oppression. But salvation has also come to his house in a rather more physical and personal form. The very fact that Jesus has invited himself to stay, has imposed himself upon the tax collector's house, gives a different but equally literal sense to the words. Salvation has come because Jesus has come, and Jesus is salvation itself.

The story of Zacchaeus is one among many examples in the Gospels of stories that illustrate the subject of this book, grace. As we shall see, grace is a word that is used in many different ways by many different people in the Christian tradition. Throughout the Bible and the history of Christianity, there are two central aspects of the word which dominate. We might distinguish between them by calling one use general, and the other specific (and that distinction is hinted at in the story of Zacchaeus – Christ is salvation itself, and Zacchaeus' changed life is the life of one who has been saved). But as soon as we speak of the grace of God we need to be careful what we say. Different ways of talking about grace can be helpful but they can also provide an unnerving combination of linguistic bog and theological minefield. We can set out two broad uses of the word grace but must not push their differences too far.

The first use tells us something about the nature of God in Christian teaching, a nature that is defined by self-giving love. The grace of God, in scripture, is over and over again the loving kindness of God towards those whom he has chosen to favour. This is seen in his relentless mercy towards his errant children and his unfailing love in the face of the faithless and loveless behaviour of those whom he has created. In this sense, the word 'grace' describes what God is like, and what God is like is self-giving love. (In Chapter 3 we will spend a little more time setting out how this idea relates to the Christian doctrine of the Trinity.) So the grace of God characterizes all that we can say about God's revelation of himself in Jesus Christ: this is what God is like. This is the God whose revelation is witnessed by the texts that we call scripture or the Bible, and proclaimed in word and deed by the Christian Church. To say, however, that grace can tell us about the nature of God is not to suggest that it is merely an attribute or a description. Love is not an attribute of God in the way that speed is an attribute of cheetahs. Love is what God is, something active and dynamic, and so grace is never simply a characteristic. We shall return to this theme.

The second basic use of the word 'grace' with which we shall concern ourselves is closely related to the first. In fact, it cannot properly be separated from it, since it is an extension of the loving mercy of God which the first use of 'grace' describes. The second idea here is that 'grace' can be used to describe a particular gift of God that enables human beings to do and be things that, left to themselves, they seem hardly able to do and be. We human beings are good at lots of things, but we are also capable of things that we are not good at achieving. A simple example is loving. Anyone who knows what it is to love can recognize in themselves an ability to be rather extraordinary, to give of oneself without condition or concern for anything other than the well-being and happiness of the object of our love. But the very awareness of our ability to love is also an awareness of our failure to do so most of the time. This awareness is an acknowledgement of the distance there is between the potential people seem to have and the reality we tend to live. Christianity teaches that this distance – we might call it the gap between our human reality and our divine potential – is bridged by the grace of God. In other words, it is overcome by the loving mercy that is God's self-giving love, and by the particular gifts to live in accordance with God's will that characterize the Christian's relationship with God in Jesus Christ.

We can and should go further with this second and particular use of the word grace. The distinctive teaching of the New Testament and of the Christian tradition is that the means by which God lifts us beyond ourselves, the gift that enables human beings to do and be more than they think they ought, is not an object or a 'power'. (By 'power' here I mean an identifiable quality that allows a person to do something previously impossible, along the lines of the effect that eating a tin of spinach has on Popeye the sailor). It is the gift whereby God unites human beings with his own life. Grace is the word we use to describe God's infinite love worked out in human beings by drawing those human beings into the perfect fellowship of the Trinity, the eternal selfless love of Father, Son and Holy Spirit. So for St Paul, as we shall see later, those who are saved by grace through faith are those who are 'in Christ', members of the Body of Christ, united with the reality of Jesus Christ crucified and risen. To receive the grace of God is to be invited into God's own self.

This language is difficult. When we use the word God we are engaging in theology, and it is sobering to remind ourselves that theologians are, by definition, those who do not know what they are talking about. The reason for this is simple. God, according to Christian teaching, is the creator. Everything that exists owes that existence, at every moment of that existence, wholly and completely, to God. When we talk of God we are creatures using created things – words – to point towards that which is infinite and ineffable. If I attempt to define God, I necessarily limit him. (Even using the pronoun 'him' is a limitation, as if God could be defined by gender.) To limit the creator to that which we know from creation really makes no sense. We understand things in the world by reason and by experience. We observe patterns of behaviour, we conclude what is true about the nature of the world through science and mathematics, we learn about ourselves and those with whom we interact through our thoughts and actions. But what direct 'experience' do we have of God? The ways in which we speak of God are indirect. Let's take the example of emotion. Human beings are often heavily influenced by their emotions, and those emotions provide us with some powerful descriptions – anger, rage, grief, desolation, for example. But human beings are limited, physical agents.

We can say, and scripture does say, some remarkable things about the love of God using the language of emotion. But this language will always be partial. It is the physical nature of humanity that gives it emotion. So it would be dangerous to assume that the same sort of language with which we express human emotions can pin down or define the God who created those human beings in all their physical limitation.

The question 'how can I know God?' is basic to humanity, we could argue, and it is a question that is answered clearly and unequivocally in Christian teaching with a name: Jesus of Nazareth. The extraordinary claim of Christianity is that the infinite and unknowable creator comes among us as a person and transforms humanity by drawing it up into a relationship with himself. 'No one has ever seen God. It is God the only son, who is close to the Father's heart, who has made him known' (John 1.18). This central notion – that God is known to us only because in the free gift of his grace he chooses to make himself known – is a model for Christian teaching on the subject of grace. Grace is what God is like – the infinite generosity that is God's self-giving love – and grace is God's gift to enable us to be like him, to unite our lives with his, and so it describes the particular characteristics of Christian life that make possible the imitation of the divine to which every Christian is called.

Before we say a little more about how these ideas are played out in the Old and New Testaments, let us turn our attention back to Zacchaeus. Grace, according to our understanding, describes the free gift of God's love. It is something that depends upon the divine initiative. For this reason, we might think that the story of Zacchaeus is an odd choice to illustrate grace. After all, does not our tiny tax collector take the initiative in this story by running on ahead and climbing the tree? No. The story depends first not on Zacchaeus clambering up his sycamore, but on Jesus coming to Jericho. The initiative, the motive force, begins with Jesus. The energy that opens our story is the energy of God, an energy to which the Gospels bear witness by their very existence, since their purpose is to encourage those who read and hear to encounter the living God come among us in Jesus of Nazareth.

Once the story has begun, once God's initiative is felt, Zacchaeus makes his first response – he ascends to his viewing platform (or rather, branch). Jesus has created a relationship between himself and Zacchaeus by entering his home town, and now Zacchaeus seeks to define that relationship by distance. He is eager to see Jesus, but he has also decided that there is safety in remaining aloof. He is a wealthy man, he does not belong among the rabble (and, as we observed earlier, he might not be safe among them anyway). Jesus has other ideas. He calls Zacchaeus down, and does so by turning on its head the notion of hospitality towards a visitor. Outrageously, he invites himself to stay at Zacchaeus' house (presumably overnight), but he issues that self-invitation in the form of a summons – he invites Zacchaeus to invite him, as it were. I *must* stay at your house today, he says ('it is necessary that I stay at your house', as the Greek puts it – there is a sense of something that is destined taking place). So Jesus characterizes the loving mercy of God by seeking out the inhabitants of Jericho, and enacts that love in drawing Zacchaeus down into his presence, enabling Zacchaeus to play host to the one he was so anxious to see, bringing it about that he and Zacchaeus are able to enjoy fellowship together.

Now, and for the second time in the story, Zacchaeus responds to Jesus. He welcomes him gladly into his home, and he announces to his guest and to any who will hear that he is a changed man. His new behaviour – overwhelmingly generous giving to those in need, and superabundant restitution to all whom he has wronged – illustrates that he is a new person. He is different from the nervous and greedy individual who was so fascinated by Jesus' coming; he has been changed by Jesus and, in particular, by the presence of Jesus. The relationship into which he has been brought by Jesus' love towards him has made it possible for Zacchaeus to do all sorts of things that would have been unthinkable only a few hours earlier.

We see, then, those two aspects of the word 'grace' at work in this story, and at work in relationship with one another. The free gift of God's love is demonstrated in the divine initiative whereby Jesus comes among the people and challenges Zacchaeus simply by his travelling through Jericho. The particular gifts of love that enable human beings to respond in accordance with the will of God are played out as the perversely topsy-turvy invitation of Jesus to Zacchaeus to play the host results in the presence of Jesus in his home, the unity of fellowship that the two enjoy, and the transformation of Zacchaeus from a person of power and wealth to a person of gratuitous love.

An under-appreciated English poet, Francis Quarles (1592–1644), reflects on this story thus:

> Methinks I see with what a busy haste
> Zacheus climbed the tree: but oh how fast
> How full of speed, canst thou imagine when
> Our saviour called he powdered down again!
> He ne'r made trial if the boughs were sound,
> Or rotten; nor how far twas to the ground.
> There was no danger feared: at such a call,

He'll venture nothing, that dare fear a fall.
Needs must he down, by such a spirit driven;
Nor could he fall, unless he fell to heaven.
Down came Zacheus, ravished from the tree;
Bird that was shot, ne'er dropped so quick as he.
(Fowler, *The New Oxford Book of Seventeenth-Century Verse*, p. 297)

Quarles recognizes that the important thing about Zacchaeus is not that he took himself up that sycamore tree, but that Jesus called him down from it. Seeing the world from a distance is one thing, and living as part of it is something else. It is the latter, the living, with which we should concern ourselves. Christians call this living 'faith' and, as we shall see, faith is not the abstract acknowledgement that something is true, but rather the response that acts as well as thinks, the consistency of life that takes seriously the love to which Christ commits us, and that orders one's life around it. This is the response to God's loving mercy, which is only possible because of God's own initiative. It is not an accident that Luke follows the story of Zacchaeus with his version of the parable of the talents (in Luke it is the parable of the pounds) in which Jesus tells of a master who entrusts three servants with his money, and returns to discover their differing responses to that trust.

Quarles's poem gives a vivid picture of Zacchaeus rushing down, with no thought for his own safety. The love of God does not invite careful response. It invites passion, excitement and enthusiasm. It invites a commitment that is unafraid to be changed. We are reminded that this story takes place in the famous city of Jericho; we all know what happens to the city of Jericho in the book of Joshua. There was nothing weak about the city walls and fortifications that caused their fall, their coming down. The blasts of the trumpets, and the shouts of the people, are the audible expression of the creative word of God, which brings the strongest things to nothing, even as it makes the nothings of this world strong. Zacchaeus, despite his lack of height, is a person of power and wealth. But he is brought to worldly nothing by the call of Jesus Christ, so as to be built up into something, to be remade in God's image, as he acts out the consequences of the love that transforms him.

All this takes place because the one who first ascended realizes the need to descend. Zacchaeus has to come down and reduce himself for the sake of God and his neighbour. Luke is fully aware that shortly in his narrative, Jesus himself will have his own ascent, and his own descent, as he mounts the instrument of execution to complete his own self-giving to the world. The gift of God's grace should not be seen apart from the self-offering of Jesus Christ.

2

Grace and the God of the Bible

Proclaiming the God of life

We began with the tale of a vertically challenged tax collector, and we saw him raised up in more ways than one. If we attend to some of the other uses of the idea of grace in scripture, we will observe that, as with the story of Zacchaeus, scripture is far more likely to show us grace than it is to define it. This is not a bad thing. Our twenty-first-century minds are desperate to tie things down by definition, but the wisdom of our forebears knew well the power of story.

In the Old Testament we associate the notion of grace, of God's loving mercy, particularly with the prophets. The poet we call Second Isaiah, for example, whose teaching we find chiefly in Isaiah 40—55, presents a dramatic announcement of God at work. He proclaims the wonderful works of the Lord, Yahweh, the God of Israel, who is bringing about the redemption and restoration of his people by liberating them from exile and captivity under the yoke of the Babylonian empire. Early in the sixth century BC, Nebuchadnezzar, King of Babylon, had besieged and conquered Jerusalem. In so doing he eventually destroyed the Temple, the dwelling place of the Lord, the place of sacrificial offering, and hence the centre of the earth as far as its worshippers were concerned. He carried off into slavery the conquered people of Judah. Speaking to those exiles, Second Isaiah promises the inversion and overthrow of worldly power, and the comfort of the Lord's own people (set memorably to music in Handel's *Messiah*). The Lord's decisive act of love towards his people will destroy those who have oppressed them, while at the same time making possible their return. This the creator achieves by bringing life where there is none, in the wilderness which they must cross to journey back west from Babylon to Jerusalem.

This theme of the life that springs out of lifelessness is basic to the prophets' insistence on the grace of Yahweh, the God of Israel. The ultimate act of grace, the deed by which the Lord is defined, is the creation of the heavens and the earth. This sets the God of Israel apart from the 'gods of the heathen' which, as the psalmist maintains, are simply idols (Psalm 96.5). The Lord, however, is the God who reigns in heaven and does whatever he pleases. What pleases him, without self-interest, is to seek out his people in love. So the Old Testament's emphasis on the Lord as the creator is married with the repeated reminder that God, having no need to create or to relate to his people, nevertheless does so because love is what God is.

The story of the Exodus is the story of the Lord's rescuing of his people from their bondage in Egypt, and forms the foundation of Israelite memory throughout the Hebrew Bible. This central theme falls squarely into the understanding of God's loving kindness we are exploring. It is because of the Lord's own actions, actions that are the free gift of his love, that his people are free to live, to worship him, and to prosper. Needless to say, his people are just that, people. And people, as we have said, are not as good at loving as they might be. The Old Testament shows us humanity in all its glory, but also in all its greed and filth and weakness. We see in the Bible the repeated turning away of God's people to worship other gods, either literal false gods or such metaphorical idols as power, wealth, sex or status. This frequent failing is almost as basic to the Old Testament narrative as is the mercy of the God who reaches out relentlessly to his stubborn and recalcitrant children. Forgiveness of sins, then, is also essential to biblical notions of grace. God gives to wrongdoers infinitely more than they deserve; despite the repeated attempts of humanity to turn its back on love, love itself just continues loving, calling and recalling people into relationship with their creator.

These themes are sometimes drawn out as extended signs and metaphors. We could point to the striking (and to some objectionable) narrative of Hosea. In that prophetic book, the love of God is compared to a faithful and loving spouse who searches for and embraces the partner whose adultery is the enactment of a fundamental infidelity. Sometimes an entire narrative is spent on characterizing God's gracious love and the extent to which it confounds others, notably those who would restrict it to some people only, or some places in particular. A famous example is the book of Jonah. It tells a tale in which the only person who fails to acknowledge and revere the universal and all-reaching love of the Lord is the prophet of the Lord himself. Often the prophetic voice will come in the form of a challenge, perhaps to the ruling authorities as one can frequently find in the book of Jeremiah. Sometimes it comes in the form of a divine address to the entire people, such as in Chapter 6 of the prophet Micah: 'O my people, what have I done to you, in what have I wearied you? Answer me!'(Micah 6.3). These words, significantly, form the beginning of the liturgical amalgamation of scriptural texts sung on Good Friday and known as 'the reproaches'.

Scriptural words for grace

The words employed in these scriptural contexts are often not words we would translate as 'grace', but are likely to belong to a family of theological terms that live closely together. These are words we translate with terms such as 'favour', 'mercy', 'steadfast love', 'kindness' or 'pity'. The Hebrew word *chen*, which we do render as 'grace', we sometimes also translate 'favour'. Another highly significant Hebrew word is *chesed*, often 'loving kindness' in English, for which the Greek word *eleos* or 'mercy' is used in the Greek Old Testament (called 'the Septuagint' because of an ancient story whereby 72 translators independently produced the same text). The former word – *chen* – is the word for which the Septuagint uses *charis*, the Greek word for grace. However, the New Testament's use of that term is closer to an amalgamation of the two Hebrew terms in question.

That Greek word '*charis*', which is the standard New Testament word for 'grace', is used in the classical period (a few centuries before the New Testament was written) in many of the ways in which we now use the English word 'grace'. It can mean outward beauty, for example, or an individual act of favour. The *charites* or 'graces' are the goddesses who grant favours such as fertility or victory; in later classical literature there are thought to be 'three graces', representing beauty, charm and goodness.

We find reflections of these varied uses in the New Testament. Luke's Gospel seems to be familiar with some sophisticated Greek writing, and the word *charis* appears in a number of different contexts, describing the favour that the young girl Mary has found with God (Luke 1.30), and the divine and human favour in which the growing Jesus increased (Luke 2.52). When those listening to Jesus, who is speaking in the Nazareth synagogue, are amazed by what he has to say, Luke tells us they are astounded by 'the gracious words that came from his mouth' (Luke 4.22). Later in the Gospel, when Jesus challenges his hearers by comparing the obligations of discipleship to a servant's duty to his master, he asks whether the master thanks the slave for doing his duty, and the Greek phrase is *echei charin?*, 'has he gratitude' or 'favour?' (Luke 17.9).

In some ancient religious uses of the word *charis*, favour is 'owed' to the gods as homage, but essential to most uses of the word in the Greek of the New Testament is the idea of gratuity. (To be sure, this is an inevitably tautological observation, since the English word 'gratuitous' takes its origin from the Latin word for grace, but the point is clear.) Favour is bestowed freely by one who is not in any way obligated to give.

The word grace in the New Testament tends to incorporate both the senses of God's active love that are contained in the Hebrew words *chen* and *chesed*: favour and loving kindness. We will look more closely at Paul's use of the word in Chapter 4, but it is worth noting immediately the connection between grace and covenant in the Old Testament, and the reception of that theological idea by the early Christian scriptures. In the Old Testament, God comes together, he enters into 'covenants' (etymologically, 'comings together') with individuals and with his chosen people. This he does for no reason other than his loving kindness towards those whom he has created. The

Hebrew scriptures tell the story of the God who initiates a relationship with his people through this coming together with Noah, Abraham, Moses and David. Through these individual covenants God comes together with the people of Israel. In the New Testament the new covenant promised in the book of Jeremiah is understood to have been enacted through the life, death and resurrection of Jesus Christ. God's grace is then, in part, the steadfast love by which God is faithful to his covenant despite the unwillingness of human beings to keep their side of the 'bargain'. But, as we noted earlier, it would be wrong to see this grace as something that simply describes a characteristic. The grace of God is understood in the Christian scriptures as something active. It is something by which God reaches out from himself in love and draws people into a relationship with himself and others. This is a relationship that can only be created by grace, and only maintained by grace.

Here we find our original distinction being developed. The grace of God can refer to the active love that initiates a relationship, but it can also refer to the gifts that allow that relationship to be sustained. This is a slightly different division from that made at the outset, 'grace' used to denote the loving kindness of God, and 'grace' used to describe a gift that enables human beings to do and be things they are unable to attain for themselves. The loving kindness of God is indeed enacted in God's enabling relationship with his people. However, Christian teaching tends to understand the grace that makes me a Christian (sometimes called sanctifying grace) as something that is a particular gift of God. It is a consequence of God's loving mercy, his grace, but it is not the same thing as that divine characteristic and activity – it is something given to me which I receive. Once received, it enables a relationship that I am then only able to maintain because of the repeated gifts of love that we sometimes call 'actual grace'. (We shall consider descriptions of grace further in later chapters.)

This difference between that which begins and that which sustains will be seen to be significant later, when we examine St Paul more closely. A preliminary glance through the Apostle's use of the word for grace, and of its relatives, shows him making frequent use of the Old Testament themes we have described. God's promise that the descendants of Abraham should inherit the world rests on grace (Romans 4.16) because it is the entirely free gift of God's love, and depends on no legal conformity. To suggest otherwise would be to attempt the impossible, to nullify the grace of God, to deny the reality of God's free gift of love (Galatians 2.21). This would be the equivalent of shutting our eyes and sticking our fingers in our ears! For Paul, the grace of God is real, whether we like it or not. That grace in which Christians stand (Romans 5.2) is the reality of a relationship, one into which believers are incorporated by being united to Christ and living in fellowship with God. The grace and peace that belong to Jesus Christ and are desired by Paul for his brother and sisters (1 Corinthians 1.3; 2 Corinthians 13.13) are the gifts of that relationship of divine love in which those who are baptized into Christ continue to live.

Stories and scandals

I began with the Gospels, and now return to them, hoping to show, through some of Luke's tales and characters in particular, the grace of God on dramatic display, something we are likely to find at least as strange as we find it comforting. Following the story of Zacchaeus is 'the parable of the pounds' (Luke 19). This is the third Gospel's version of the 'parable of the talents' in Matthew 25. Rather than three servants who are given three different amounts, Luke has ten people each of whom are given a pound – around three months' wages in one go. Like so many of Jesus' parables, this story is not a tale of warmth or security, but a challenge to respond to the gifts with which God blesses his people. Striking for our purposes, however, is the ending. The person who has turned his pound into ten pounds is given the one pound taken from the worthless servant. The narrator is well aware of the seeming scandal, and has the other characters object. But the man of power is adamant: 'I tell you, to all those who have, more will be given; but from those who have nothing, even what they have will be taken away' (Luke 19.26). These alarming words make little sense until we insert into our mental picture some sort of basket or container. If I have a basket to contain my apples, for example, I can easily accommodate more apples. If I am struggling to hold a few apples in my hands, then the addition of more apples will likely cause me to drop the lot. There is a connection to be made between this parable and the ways of thinking about grace that we identified above. If something has been started, if I have something to begin with, then more can be built. If a relationship has been initiated, it can be sustained and grown. If no such beginning has taken place, no amount of sustenance can maintain something that is not there.

In the first Gospel to be written, that of Mark, Jesus begins his ministry proclaiming that 'The time is fulfilled, and the kingdom of God has come near; repent, and believe in the good news' (Mark 1.15). That good news is the unconditional love of God, the free gift of God's grace, by which all are invited to partake of the Kingdom, the new reign of God that is being inaugurated in Jesus. Time and again through the Gospels we encounter the proclamation of God's love as something that confounds our expectations, reverses our earthly orders and hierarchies and defies our presuppositions and prejudices. The parable of the workers in the vineyard comes to mind (Matthew 20.1–16): those who have worked all day understandably expect to be paid more than those who turned up at the last minute, but the free gift of God is not governed by rules of equity. The natural human reaction at this point is the child's complaint, 'It's not fair', but human whining unwittingly hits the spot. It is not fair, the love of God is absolutely not 'fair'. If it were, it would be given to those who deserve it, but infinite love cannot be deserved by finite creatures. Thus, we can truly say there is no 'fairness' involved where God's grace is concerned. Turning again to Luke we might observe that, in human terms, the elder brother of the prodigal son is perfectly justified in complaining when his wastrel of a younger brother is welcomed home, and wined and dined. What is being demonstrated in these stories is not fairness, not justice in any sense with which we are familiar, but the unreasonable and inexhaustible love of God which is the free gift of his grace.

The gospel writers, Luke in particular, will offend us if we expect social acceptability. Ideas of invitation and hospitality, for example, are developed in narrative form to challenge our assumptions about what and who might be thought good or deserving. In Luke 7, Simon the Pharisee has invited Jesus to his house. No doubt he had gone to great trouble (or had servants go to great trouble for him). He will have been looking forward to hosting Jesus, a man who seemed to attract attention wherever he went. As the host, Simon will have expected to spend the evening in a position of authority, the one in charge of all that takes place. But, instead, in comes an anonymous woman. (She is not Mary Magdalen, incidentally, she is anonymous: unnamed but not unnoticed.) She knows nothing of decorum, but throws herself weeping at Jesus, dripping her salty tears on to his dusty feet, and wiping those feet dry with the mess of her hair, before compounding that mess with the ointment on which she had spent her last penny. Simon, the reader assumes, would say she does not belong in his house. She threatens his control of the situation, she threatens his reputation, and the kudos he is gaining by having this famous young man to dinner. In other words, she is spoiling all his carefully laid plans.

Simon's command of events is at an end. He thought he knew what he was doing, but now his assumptions are challenged. He now doubts his conviction that Jesus is a prophet – the reason he is making such a fuss of him – because were Jesus a prophet he would know that this woman is a sinner. All his plans and expectations have been turned on their head. The reader or the hearer of the gospel is able to grasp the contrast, and recognize that Simon the Pharisee was never in charge in the first place. Jesus is in fact the host in this situation. Simon's difficulty is not that Jesus is not a prophet, but that he, Simon, has not listened to him. A prophet is one who speaks the word of the Lord. The woman is certainly a sinner, but everybody is a sinner, and everybody is the object of God's unconditional and forgiving love. Which of two people will love more? One who has just been bought a pint of beer, or one who has just had a lifetime of debts cancelled? Jesus tells Simon this story to bring him up short.

Not only is Simon deluded about the love of God, he is also, ironically, deluded about how to behave. He, the social master, the founder of the feast who has gone to so much trouble to get everything right, has actually got everything wrong. By his words, Jesus gives Simon a lesson in etiquette. It is the woman who has washed Jesus' feet, and greeted him with a kiss, and anointed him before his meal. All these are the right things to do, and all of them have been done by this embarrassing intruder, who has shamed the social snobs for whom shame is the worst fate of all. Simon thinks that if Jesus were a prophet, he would know if someone were a sinner. Yet if only Simon the Pharisee had known himself to be a sinner (rather than condemning the woman as one), then this dog's dinner of an occasion would be perfectly fitting. In this case, he would know how to respond to the love of God when it was sitting at his table and staring him in the face.

Also unique to Luke is another pompous official and awkward and inconvenient woman. In Luke 18, Jesus tells a story of an unjust judge who is repeatedly petitioned for justice by a widow, for whom he has no care or regard. He answers her suit in the end simply to give himself an easier time: 'Though I have no fear of God and no respect for anyone, yet because this widow keeps bothering me, I will grant her justice, so that she may not wear me out by her continual coming' (Luke 18.4–5). The word 'continual' here could be translated 'in the end'. In the end she will wear me out by her coming. The judge is sufficiently aware of the situation to realize that he will falter before the widow does. More important is the phrase 'she will wear me out'. This Greek verb – *hupopiazo* – actually means to give someone a black eye. It appears in I Corinthians when Paul is talking about fighting, pummelling himself to keep his body under control. It is used in Aristotle to refer to a straightforward punch in the eye. So the sense we need to hold on to here is something like 'she will beat me black and blue by her coming'. The judge is being battered by this extraordinary woman.

It is here, unexpectedly, that the unjust judge and the gracious mercy of God are at their closest. The widow keeps coming back, keeps buffeting the judge, rather like a boxer who batters a punchball, sees it swing back, bashes it back again, and so forth. This really is persistence, and thank goodness that the punchball keeps swinging back, for so does the love of God. We human beings batter our creator with our requests, with our desires, with our mistakes, our half-truths, our splendid isolation from the needs of those around us. Yet again and again he is there to be hit, his love swings back and swings back again, undiminished, unabated and unrelenting.

This lovely little boxing metaphor has almost been slipped in unseen, but it leads the reader to a further and more striking comparison with which this parable challenges the presuppositions we bring to the idea of God's grace. The widow is persistent, never giving up. The gospel is a reminder that the people of God ought also to be persistent. The fact is, however, that most of the time we are not. Far from continual, far from unending, our prayer and our worship is apt to be minimal, slight and insignificant. Some of the time it seems our only consistent behaviour is in trying to resist the love of God. God, on the other hand, is persistence itself. It is not we who are bothering God with our concerns, but he who is bothering us, not with blows and buffets, but with quiet, insistent promptings. The grace of God is always enquiring, questioning, and daring us to respond. However firmly we fasten the bolt, the love of God will seep in under the door, gnawing at us, eating slowly into us, gently suggesting itself in our world and our worship, in those we love and those who are strangers, in word and sacrament, in prayer and in people.

The shape of the cross

The contrasts that confront us again and again in Luke's Gospel allow us to go further in answering our initial question, 'What is grace?' There is one more thing to say, and that one more thing is – literally – crucial. In Christian theology, grace is cruciform. Grace is that which crosses humanity, which acts both in contradistinction to it and in relationship with it. The image of two lines intersecting at right angles, the image of a cross, is one that Christian artists, poets and musicians have not been slow to employ, and we shall examine some examples later on. For now we can complete this introduction simply by holding on to the image. We begin with a straight line, horizontal or vertical. And we add to it another line, crossing at right angles. That line contrasts with the first, it opposes its direction. But it also intersects with it, creating something new, making through the relationship of the two lines the form we call a cross. Grace is cruciform because the love of God both contradicts the weakness of human fear and self, and transforms that weakness by making a new relationship, and thus remaking human beings by uniting human life with the life of God.

If we find this image helpful, we might add to it another. A crucifix, a representation not just of the cross form itself, but of Christ crucified – either a representation of his passion and suffering, or a depiction of Christ the King reigning from the throne which is his cross – presents us with another strikingly simple sight: the open arms of Jesus, welcoming the beholder into his embrace. Grace is cruciform because it crosses human life, but also because it invites human life in, stretches out its arms to enfold the beholder and to offer the beholder a share in the embrace with which the Father holds the Son who is closest to his own self.

Grace is the love of God at work, uniting human beings with Jesus Christ, the second person of the Trinity incarnate, and drawing them into fellowship with him. It is not neat and tidy, not polite and withdrawn, but gently and relentlessly aggressive, offending us with its inclusion and undermining our securest assumptions about that which we think we know to be true. The subject matter of this book is not an academic debate but the indescribable reality of God in action, an action whose beginning and end is located within the life of God himself. To that life and that location we now turn.

3

Grace and the Christian doctrine of God

Christianity teaches not abstract but particular things. It teaches the particular claim that God became a human being and lived as a particular person in a particular time and place. In expressing this, the Christian Church also teaches a particular doctrine of God. We call that teaching the doctrine of the Trinity, the teaching that God is three persons in one substance (a phrase that I shall consider more fully below). Christians encounter the life of God through grace because this is an encounter initiated and enabled by God, not by any human endeavour. God takes the initiative, and God's initiative is not something that should be seen as an added extra in Christian reflection on God and the world. It is easy to think of God as basically something singular, but this is not Christian thought. What we are talking about here is what it means to be divine. The self-giving love of God that unites our lives with his is the outpouring of God's life. Human beings are invited to share that life through grace. The Christian doctrine of grace relies entirely upon the Christian doctrine of the Trinity, as this chapter will make clear.

The doctrine of the Trinity is the Christian doctrine of God. There is a standing joke among clergy that one wants to avoid preaching on Trinity Sunday, because talking about the Trinity is the hardest of theological tasks. This is both true and false. It is true, because adequate talk of God is impossible. But it is more importantly false, because talk of the Trinity is just Christian talk about God, not some additional complication. That is why the rather lame trick of demonstrating the Trinity by having one person wear three different hats is so misleading. Christians do not believe first in a unitary idea and then clothe that one idea with three different costumes. Rather, Christianity teaches that God is nothing other than an eternal relationship of love, a perfect community of self-giving which we call Father, Son and Holy Spirit. Christian talk of grace cannot be separated from Christian talk of God.

Here our choice of words must be even more careful than usual. Some people are good at chess. Some people are witty and entertaining. Some people are brilliant with cars. Different people have different characteristics. But talk of God is not talk about the characteristics God happens to have, as if God might have been a pianist or a diplomat or a double-glazing salesman. It is not the case that God happens to be loving, if by that we mean something analogous to the way that some human beings happen to be good at certain things – Lionel Messi at football, for example. It is rather the case that love is what God is. All Christian talk of God encountered in Jesus Christ is talk of God as love.

The self-emptying of God

In a justly famous passage from his letter to the Philippians, St Paul invites his hearers and readers to model themselves upon Christ 'who, though he was in the form of God, did not regard equality with God as something to be exploited, but emptied himself, taking the form of a slave, being born in human likeness. And being found in human form, he humbled himself and became obedient to the point of death – even death on a cross' (Philippians 2.6–8). It is worth noting just how extraordinary this text is in its historical context. This is Paul, formerly Saul, a man who by his own admission was a Pharisee, a pious and zealous child of the tribe of Benjamin; and he is writing of a fellow Jew, a teacher and preacher whom he never met, one who was executed as a criminal only 30 years before. And Paul says, of the teacher he never met, that he was in the form of God. We need not know much about history to think this remarkable.

Translations of the New Testament tended until recently to translate these words slightly differently: the common reading was something like Jesus 'did not think equality with God something to be grasped', presumably implying that it might be something to be snatched at, to be rudely and greedily seized as an ill-mannered child would grab at a sweet or a present. There is sense in this wording but our version offers the translation, 'Did not regard equality with God as something to be *exploited*'. This rendering, 'exploited', or taken advantage of, is an idiomatic usage which a number of Pauline scholars have noticed is paralleled in other late Greek texts. It also fits both the context and Paul's wider teaching about Christ absolutely perfectly. Jesus did not regard equality with God as something of which to take advantage.

The most interesting phrase, however, is contained in the words 'emptied himself'. From that excerpt we take the name for a significant tradition of talk about Christ, talk that we call kenotic Christology, kenotic because of the

Greek word *kenōsis,* which means 'emptying'. The use of this idea in Philippians is considered so important that the word *kenōsis* is a word that every student of theology would understand (whether or not the student knew Greek). The importance of this idea for some is the contention that, in becoming human, the Son empties himself of his divinity, only to take it up again after his passion, death and resurrection. This image of 'kenotic Christology' has many advocates, often those inspired by the great German Reformer Martin Luther. In the nineteenth and twentieth centuries, and in British theology in particular as well as German, it was held to offer something of a solution to traditional problems in talking about Jesus as both human and divine. If Jesus emptied himself of divinity, then worrying about certain theological puzzles, such as whether or not the historical Jesus knew all the truths of mathematics, as some theologians have, seems even less worthwhile than it already might (and – let's face it – it didn't seem terribly worthwhile to begin with).

This idea can – if taken too far – be problematic. When Christ emptied himself, he did not empty himself of his divinity. God cannot cease to be God: that much is logically impossible, as nonsensical as the idea that God can create a four-sided triangle. The incarnate Son retains his divine nature throughout. What that means in more helpful terms is that it is always true to say, 'this man Jesus is God.' If we take this notion of emptying where it should not go, we will end up saying that it was not actually God who became human. We will find ourselves talking of some lesser being who was not quite God, who accommodated himself so as to become human, leaving his divinity safely behind in heaven. Such is the danger of the idea of kenosis in Christian theology.

More recently, other theologians have observed that the kenosis, the emptying, that Paul talks of is better considered as a pattern of the whole life of God. What it means to be divine *is* to be 'kenotic', emptying. Not the emptying of divinity into something that is not divine, but the eternal emptying of each of the three persons of the Trinity into the others. There is nothing about the Father that is not always being poured out in love to the Son and the Spirit, and the same is true of those two. What God *is* is a life of self-giving love, a life of self-emptying quite regardless of humanity, creation or incarnation. But as the great German theologian Karl Barth reminds us, God has chosen to be *God for us*. God in the freedom of his love has chosen to unite himself with humanity, has chosen to work love out in the outflowing actions of creation and redemption, to empty divinity not just within himself but outside himself, into our world and our lives, as if emptying an endless vessel of love into the hearts of those who fear the risk of genuinely loving another.

When coming to the Gospels, readers are often struck by the particular character of the passion narratives, those rich and compelling meditations upon the last days of Jesus' life and the offering of his life in perfect love. In Philippians 2, Paul is setting out his own little passion narrative, a poetic expression of that which gives each of the Gospels its climax and meaning. The stories of Jesus' passion are the drama of the kenosis, this self-emptying which is the revelation to each of us of the true life of God. Jesus' relentless march towards Jerusalem, his agonized struggle in the garden, his patient endurance in the face of breathless death, his seemingly ridiculous words of forgiveness as the nails pierce his skin and the oxygen is sucked from within his lungs, all the events of his suffering and death are the events of the one who was in the form of God emptying himself, taking the form of a servant and becoming obedient unto death, even death on a cross. The Gospels, in their concentration on this, the most basic of all Christian stories, summarize by Jesus' self-sacrifice and death the narrative they have been concerned with throughout. It is the narrative history of God, of divine self-giving. The Christian teaching that Jesus is God incarnate is the articulation of the Christian doctrine of God in a human context. God gives himself to the world by uniting that world to himself, by becoming a human being and drawing creation into the community of love.

Love without self

So then, the love of God incarnate in Jesus Christ is the beginning and end of the Christian doctrine of God, the teaching we call Trinitarianism. Discussion of the Trinity often falls victim to the mistaken assumption that it is when speaking of God as Father, Son and Holy Spirit that the abilities of human reason have come to an end of their usefulness. The idea here, presumably, is that the notion of one God is comprehensible but three persons in one God is incomprehensible. This is a serious red herring. As I argued earlier, the nature of God – what it means to be divine – is not something we can circumscribe or understand. To think we can define God is as misguided as to think we can have a conversation with a tree: it's a thought that shows we have misunderstood our subject. For God to be comprehensible, God would have to be something that exists within the framework we call the world, or everything, or creation. But God is not 'part' of anything, but rather the source of everything. Hence God is no more mysterious once we start speaking of him as three persons. Such talk might also cause us to think that discussion of the Trinity is essentially abstract, with little or nothing to do with the realities of Christian life. On the contrary, however, if the Trinity is the life of God, it can never be abstract, and can only be active.

All this is not to say that the Church's encounter with God in Jesus Christ does not provoke questions. (This is a book about theology, after all!) These questions include puzzles as to how best to speak about Jesus Christ in two seemingly contrasting aspects. If we think that Jesus is truly human and truly divine then we will surprise ourselves by our ability to make some remarkable statements: Jesus raised the dead or Jesus was omnipotent; God was born, God suffered and died, and so on. The basis of these statements is what is often called the doctrine of the two natures. The word 'nature' describes what something is, and answers the question 'What?' In the case of Jesus, two answers are correct: Jesus was both human and divine. Hence we can say of Jesus that he did divine things, or of God that he did human things. These statements present their own problems – for instance, how, if God was dying on a cross, is it also true that the creator was sustaining the universe? Such problems, arising from the early Church's reading of scripture and the talk of Father, Son and Spirit which it found there, are the problems of God-talk that Trinitarian theology addresses.

Practical theology

The doctrine of the Trinity is an articulation of the truth that the life of God is a life of self-giving love and nothing else. What it means to be divine, then, is completely and exhaustively to be given to another in love. The three things we call divine – Father, Son and Holy Spirit – are three 'persons' who are literally self-less. There is nothing of self in the persons of the Trinity that is not always and eternally being offered to another. When we think of relationships of love we think of physical persons separated by spatial and biological matter. These physical persons can nevertheless unite themselves to other physical persons in love (and can, for example, express that unity in the physicality of sexual relationships). But the persons of the Trinity cannot exist apart from one another, as if that comes first and then they choose to enter into loving relationship as human beings do. They are essentially related, which is to say that they cannot be themselves without being related – it is part of their *essence*. And we need to say more. The persons of the Trinity are, as Christian theology puts it, *subsistently* related – they exist in relationships so perfect that nothing other than relatedness gives the persons, the divine lovers, their identity. These relationships support themselves. The doctrine of the Trinity challenges us to imagine the possibility of self-giving love so perfect that there is nothing left behind, no remainder or residue of self, only the act of love that is offered to another.

That pattern of self-giving love is lived out in the person of Jesus of Nazareth. It is by starting with Christ that we can begin to understand the practical consequences of the Trinitarian life. The orthodox teaching that Christ was one person in two natures – one individual, both human and divine – is the framework within which we are able to understand the twofold character of Jesus' life and mission. This twofold character is seen in his loving obedience to the Father, and his loving compassion for his fellow humans.

The obedience of the Son to the will of the Father is not different from the Son's offering of his own life for those around him: both are the enfleshment, the incarnation, of the love of God. If we centre our attention upon Christ, we can then see love poured out in these two directions – love for the Father, love for his children. Jesus answers the question, 'Which is the greatest commandment of all?', with a twofold response: love the Lord your God with all your heart, with all your soul, with all your mind and with all your strength; and love your neighbour as yourself (Mark 12.29–31). The coupling of two loves – love for God, love for one another – is the most important guide to life and action.

Grace and fellowship with the divine

If we return to our twofold definition of grace we can begin to see, I hope, what this has to do with the doctrine of the Trinity. Grace as expressive of what God is like – the loving kindness of God, as the Bible has it – is not a different description or claim about divine love than the doctrine of the Trinity itself. God is self-giving love. And grace as the gift by which God unites human lives to his draws human beings into the life of the Trinity itself. This is the means by which human beings are enabled to be that much more than their own selves will permit. Being united to Christ means being offered to the Father in love. The saving act of God and the grace of God experienced by those who live the Christian life are the same thing. They are the enticement, the seduction of divine fellowship, into whose divine selflessness the selfishness of humanity is brought.

This fellowship is the result of grace. When we speak of grace we speak of the selfless love of God, and hence we commit ourselves to the peculiarly Christian insight that God is Trinity. But we should not be content to leave things there, because it cannot be emphasized enough that the doctrine of the Trinity is not one aspect of Christian teaching among others, but the foundation on which all Christian doctrine stands. The doctrine of grace flows from the doctrine of the Trinity because all Christian teaching is generated by that origin. In this respect, we can speak of the essential unity of Christian teaching, because there is no aspect of Christian theology that cannot be located, in some sense, in the claim that the life of God is a life of perfect self-giving love.

We can see this in the 'big' subjects of Christian theology. The teaching that God is creator, for example, is the teaching that God's selfless love overflows, loves in excess as it were, beyond the divine life to bring the world into being. God does not 'make' the world, in the sense that making involves starting with something and forming it into something else. Rather, the love of God brings something from nothing. The love of God acts freely, without constraint, for no reason and with no explanation. There is no answer to the question 'Why did God create?' other than the love which God is. But the same applies to what is, differently, called the doctrine of salvation, the claim that God in his love acts to restore humanity and bring it into relationship with himself. We rightly say that God *divinizes* humanity. God raises humanity to his own life so that human persons can participate in the perfect love of the Trinity, because in the incarnation humanity is drawn into the life of God and offered perfectly and eternally by the Son to the Father. We shall spell this out in more detail in the next chapters.

Here, we must simply be aware that creation and redemption are not acts of divine caprice, as if God wakes up in the morning wondering what to do today. (With imaginative anarchy, Eddie Izzard's show *Glorious* presents just that possibility, with God pointing out to his imaginary mother that he can't miss the best part of the day by lying in bed, because he hasn't created the best part of the day yet!) Creation and redemption are two sides of the same coin, and that coin is the nature of God, the life of love, which is Trinitarian first and last.

These 'big' subjects, then, mirror what we have to say about grace. All Christian doctrine is reflection upon the loving act of the God of love. It is no coincidence that the only appearance of the phrase 'Father, Son and Holy Spirit' in the New Testament comes in the risen Jesus' instructions to his followers to make disciples of all nations, baptizing them in the name of the Father and of the Son and of the Holy Spirit. The meaning of grace is that God's love does the work for us. As Christians are baptized in the name of Father, Son and Holy Spirit, the Church enacts, in the form of a sign, what God is doing. The God who created and sustains the world unites himself with humanity in Christ to offer that which human beings could not offer for themselves – a perfect life of human love – so that all humanity can live in the continuing power and presence of the Spirit who gives new life to the people of God. Baptism is a threefold action, a threefold dying and rising, an entering of Christ's tomb on the Friday, existing in the void of human death on the Saturday, and finally on the Sunday bursting up and out into the eternal life of the Trinity.

We identify God's giving of himself in love with the 'mission' of the Son and the Spirit – those who are 'sent', like the apostles – to enact divine love in the world. This self-giving is the working out in our world of what is already true about God himself. What the Christian doctrine of the Trinity teaches is that God is always and eternally giving himself completely in love to another, in the eternal motion, the eternal and energetic action, which is the life of Father, Son and Spirit. This self-giving, this pouring out of life and love into our world and into our hearts, is the saving act of God, and the Christian doctrine of grace is an attempt to give content to that action and its consequences. By grace, human beings are baptized into the death and resurrection of Christ and incorporated, brought into his body, to enjoy true fellowship, true relationship with the God who is Father, Son and Holy Spirit.

Grace in poetic conversation

We can see this Trinitarian understanding of grace at work if we compare and contrast two popular and wonderful pieces from the golden age of English poetry in the early modern period. Both are saturated with threefold imagery, both describe the initiative of divine love and the reluctance of human engagement, but one, much more than the other, demonstrates the grace of God that brings the recipient into a life of relationship with Father, Son and Spirit.

> Batter my heart, three-person'd God; for you
> As yet but knock; breathe, shine, and seek to mend;
> That I may rise, and stand, o'erthrow me, and bend
> Your force, to break, blow, burn, and make me new.
> I, like an usurp'd town, to another due,
> Labour to admit you, but O, to no end.
> Reason, your viceroy in me, me should defend,

But is captived, and proves weak or untrue.
Yet dearly I love you, and would be loved fain,
But am betroth'd unto your enemy;
Divorce me, untie, or break that knot again,
Take me to you, imprison me, for I,
Except you enthrall me, never shall be free,
Nor ever chaste, except you ravish me. (Donne, *John Donne*, pp. 177–8)

Perhaps the most famous of John Donne's *Holy Sonnets*, this stunning poem is a prayer. Donne pleads with the Triune God to take possession of his self by force. His entreaty is a series of violent images which speak of resistance and conquest. The poet, a representative of fallen humanity, compares himself to a town under siege, and a lover enslaved to someone else. His desire to belong to God is frustrated by his inability to act in accordance with that desire. He cannot do what he knows to be right. The divine initiative, however, is the key to his salvation. The insistence with which the love of God works both within and without to transform an enemy into a friend is a description of the grace of God. That perfect love might seek relationship with that so firmly opposed to it, is as contrary a notion as the poet can imagine. Hence, in good biblical style, he expresses the transformation that God brings about in a powerful collection of opposites. He cannot be free unless imprisoned by God; he cannot be pure unless the love of God takes him in passionate union.

Notice that the sonnet begins with a knock at the door, or, rather, a hammering at the door, of the sort music lovers find at the beginning of Beethoven's Fifth Symphony. The words 'Batter my heart' give us four syllables, three short and one long, as if beaten out with a fist on a sturdy oak. The following words, 'three-person'd God', also offer four syllables, but this time broader, each sound delineated so that three separate knocks resolve into a fourth. So it is that in six words, and eight syllables, the poet enunciates better than any theological book the Christian doctrine of the Trinity. The god to whom Donne prays is not an abstract metaphysical deity, but the God of Christianity – Father, Son and Holy Spirit – the perfect relationship of love which is the basis of Christian talk about divinity.

For the poet, the explicit mention of the 'three-person'd God' makes more powerful his theme of assault, battery and conquest. The Christian is attacked on every side, as it were, by Father, Son and Spirit. But the very violence of the poem might suggest a more straightforward one-to-one opposition that can only go so far in speaking to us of the love of God. We might observe that the relational language in this poem is not just aggressive but even abusive. Whether we like that or not, and the reader is free to decide, there is something else inescapable about these lines. The fact is, Donne is telling God what to do. His prayer is couched as an instruction, as if God is failing to possess him because he – God – is not doing things quite as well as he might. To be sure, much prayer in scripture and the Christian tradition appears to tell God certain things, and it does not seem odd. But Donne seems to be saying, 'Do it like this, because at the moment you are doing it like that.' God, we might think, is getting it wrong: if only God acted as Donne wants him to act, presumably everything would be as it should!

The oddity of this marvellous poem becomes clear when we read it alongside another marvellous, and equally famous, English poem which speaks of the grace of God. This one is by Donne's contemporary, George Herbert:

Love bade me welcome, yet my soul drew back
Guilty of dust and sin.
But quick-eyed Love, observing me grow slack
From my first entrance in,
Drew nearer to me, sweetly questioning,
If I lack'd any thing.

A guest, I answerd, worthy to be here:
Love said, You shall be he.
I the unkind, ungrateful? Ah, my dear,
I cannot look on thee.
Love took my hand, and smiling did reply,
Who made the eyes but I?

Truth, Lord, but I have marr'd them: let my shame
Go where it doth deserve.
And know you not, says Love, who bore the blame?
My dear, then I will serve.
You must sit down, says Love, and taste my meat
So I did sit and eat.

(Herbert, *The Complete English Poems*, p. 178)

Donne announces his Trinitarian faith with the three-into-one sounds that begin his poem. Herbert, more quietly, gives his lines a Trinitarian name, 'Love: III'. As with Donne's knocking, this is a poem of divine initiative. Love welcomes the writer, who instinctively backs away, knowing that he is, as he puts it, 'guilty of dust and sin'. These two nouns are telling. Dust is the biblical word for humanity – the name 'Adam' means both 'man' and 'dust' – and set alongside the less surprising word sin, it is surely intended by Herbert, and to indicate that he, as any Christian, is in need of the grace of God not only because he is guilty of particular sins, but because as a human being he cannot survive without God. Theologians call this notion the doctrine of original sin, and I shall say more about it in a future chapter.

In the poem, the reversion of the Christian soul is contrasted strongly but gently with the swift persistence of grace. As often as the poet draws back, the God of love reaches further and further towards him in order to draw him into fellowship. The structure of each line displays this interaction. With each mention of the activity of love, there is a lengthening of that activity. To begin with, love is given only half a line – 'Love bade me welcome'; this half-line is then contrasted with the backsliding of the soul that is guilty. But love's next mention goes further, beyond the half-line, as far as the end of the word 'observing', and finally, responding to the limp and lifeless soul, love fills an entire line, 'Drew nearer to me, sweetly questioning'. This is theological word painting at its best – with every attempt of ours to back away from the love of God, that love reaches further and further so as to complete the embrace that is its goal.

That threefold reaching reminds us of Father, Son and Spirit, but the poem's three verses also make the point. The first verse is the verse of divine initiative. From nothing God brings something, an invitation to relationship, an enticement to love. The second verse expresses human unwillingness to accept that love, and the earthly complaint that we do not belong in the arms of the creator, having marred his image and spurned his love. But that love, according to the Christian gospel, is personified for us as a human being, Jesus of Nazareth, and hence the transformation that we resist is already anticipated and achieved in the perfect representative of humanity to the Father. Our seeming inability to accept and respond to this great truth is the subject of the third verse, the verse in which the work of God within us, the breath of life which is the Holy Spirit, allows us to enjoy genuine fellowship with the divine.

When that fellowship is achieved, we observe that the conversation between love and its reluctant guest has come to an end of its questioning. Throughout the poem, love answers the guest not with answers but with questions, enticing him to recognize the truth that is leading him. The guest talks not of seeing but of looking. We might be reminded of Isaiah, or the Gospel of Mark where the prophet is quoted: 'they may indeed look, but not perceive, and may indeed listen, but not understand' (Mark 4.12, quoting Isaiah 6.9). The difference between looking and perceiving challenges us to reflect that while the presence of God in the world provides the greatest of all sights, it also results in the greatest possible blindness. Those who are blind to the existence of truth can, by definition, know nothing. When the enquiries of love come to an end, the poet suggests he has come to the realization of the true order of things, 'my dear, then I will serve', only to be told by love – told at last and not asked – that he must sit down and partake of love's feast. That conversation is our own. Our inclination, our half-recognition, is to acknowledge God by falling down on our faces and offering service. But the God we acknowledge is the one already serving us at table. The poet only finally enjoys love's welcome when he is enabled to understand that which makes no sense to him – that the God who is his maker is also his servant – and then can sit and be nourished by that which is spread before him.

41

Why contrast these two poems? Both are glorious examples of Christian verse, both inspire and engage, and both have been read and prayed by English-speaking Christians for centuries. I suggest not a value judgement between two very different pieces of writing, but simply an observation that here we have two poems about grace, both thoroughly Trinitarian in content, but offering rather opposing models of divine action. Where Donne's Christian feels the need to be bludgeoned into submission, Herbert's baffled and hesitant guest plays out a dance with God, in which his backward steps are always outpaced by the divine footsteps forward, and he is gently but firmly drawn into the relationship of love which he tries so hard to resist. While Donne's Christian is dominated and defeated, Herbert's is fed in fellowship with the divine.

Being alive

A final analogue takes us away from theological poetry and into untheological music (if music can ever be 'untheological'). Stephen Sondheim's groundbreaking musical *Company*, first performed in 1970, was originally entitled *Threes*. Through a series of episodic scenes and musical numbers, revolving around the central character Bobby and his thirty-fifth birthday, it describes the life of a successful and still young middle-class single New Yorker whose friends are all well used to marriage and to relationships (many times over in some cases), while he, Bobby, seems unable to commit. The opening music, which recurs as a motif throughout the show, consists in the repeated calling of Bobby's name, in different forms by different friends (Bobby, Bobby, Bobby baby, Bobby bubi, Robby, Robert darling) and moves to a chorus in which a series of short staccato monosyllables are brought to completion with the three syllables of the word 'company' (Sondheim, *Finishing the Hat*, p. 170):

> Phone rings,
> door chimes,
> in comes company.
> No strings
> Good times
> Room hums, company.

In this chorus, the monosyllables are all on a single note, while the word 'company' is a short rising scale of three notes. Among many other things, the song communicates the strangeness of Bobby's single life, where he is repeatedly making up a three, coming together with couples whom he knows and loves, but who themselves might be using him for distraction or contrast or projection of who knows what problems of their own.

At the end of the show, Bobby sings the climactic number, 'Being alive', a song that reflects his journey from a fear of commitment and relationship to a desire to take the risk of love and become fully the person he has the potential to be, by daring to make himself vulnerable to another.

> Somebody need me too much
> Somebody know me too well
> Somebody pull me up short
> And put me through hell
> And give me support
> For being alive
> Make me alive . . .

The final verse ends with these lines:

> Somebody crowd me with love
> Somebody force me to care
> Somebody let me come through
> I'll always be there
> As frightened as you
> To help us survive
> Being alive, being alive,
> Being alive! (Sondheim, *Finishing the Hat*, p. 195)

As these concluding words are sung, the musical theme used at the very beginning of the show for the word 'company' returns, underneath the principal melody. And then, in the final notes, the three notes of 'company' return to the fore. Only, this final time, it is not a rising scale, but a descending one, a scale that comes home to its final cadence and settles into completion as Bobby rejoices in the discovery that truly to be alive is to love and to live in relationship.

This musical example helps us not because it relies upon bringing together three and one specifically (though it does no harm for Trinitarian theology to be reminded that aural communication is often fuller than visual), but because of the manner in which Sondheim manages to harmonize individuality and relationship by drawing the individual into a fellowship that makes him more fully the individual he has the potential to be. The music, enfolding twos and threes into one, and then reversing the open-ended theme of the beginning to create a sense of coming home and being at last fully oneself, both poses a question and answers it, draws us towards the answer as the divine host invites Herbert's sinner into table fellowship with him.

To contrast and then enfold one with three is to repeat our image of grace as cruciform. Bobby's need for fellowship crosses, contradicts, his commitment-free single life. He discovers that the fellowship that he so fears will in fact realize the many possibilities within himself that are currently lying dormant, and so it is the joining of the contrast, the wrapping of fellowship around singularity, that allows the music, and the musical, to come to its challenging conclusion. Grace confounds us, but it embraces us as well.

4

Christ, grace and justification

When Christians do theology, St Paul is never far from the scene. Many people associate the use of the word grace in Christian thought almost exclusively with the letters of Paul in the New Testament, and with debates in Christian history that centre on the interpretation of those letters. This is not an unreasonable view, since not only is Paul very fond of using the word grace – *charis* – when setting out his understanding of God's saving act in Christ, he also imbues the word with a particular theological richness that goes beyond the simple ideas of free gift and God's loving mercy. Paul does not think of grace as something abstract, something that is true about God, just something that helps us describe God as we might use references to hair colour or temperament when we try to describe a person to a stranger. As we have seen in the previous chapters, Christian notions of grace are rooted in something active, something dynamic – the unceasing self-giving love that is our best articulation of the unknowable life of God. This understanding of grace begins, in Christian theology, with Paul.

The story of Paul offers a way into the dynamism of grace. In one of the most familiar biblical tales (a tale told, incidentally, three times in three slightly different ways in the Acts of the Apostles) we hear of Saul of Tarsus, a young man who was a leading figure in early attempts to suppress the apostles' message of God's salvation through Jesus Christ. On his way to the metropolis of Damascus, to further his attempts to silence those who proclaimed Jesus to be God's Messiah, Saul was confronted by a blinding light and heard the voice of Jesus asking him, 'why do you persecute me?' That moment transformed Saul's entire life, and we now refer to those events as the 'conversion of St Paul'.

It is worth noticing, however, that to begin with Saul – given the new name Paul to go with his new identity as a Christian – can do very little, because the light of Christ's presence has blinded him. The light on the road leaves him unable to see; he staggers to Damascus led by the hand of his companion, and is received and finally rescued by the Christian disciple Ananias. Light can be a dangerous thing. Following his vision, Saul's perception is dazzled. Illumination is essential, but it is also risky. Light without the protection of shade can actually damage, rather than enable, our vision. One who lives for years in the darkness of a cave will find that his eyes take a very long time to adjust. He is, in the interim, simply blind. If all we are given is a blinding flash of light, we are very unlikely to have our perception and understanding improved. When we use the word grace we are right to resist any tendency to think of it as merely an abstract characteristic of God. It is love in action, in motion towards and within us. But we should also beware of thinking only of a single moment, a one-off experience, at which everything changes, the world is turned on its head and suddenly all makes sense. Christian discipleship suggests a rather different model. When in the Gospels Jesus calls those he wishes to follow him, he does not stop and explain why. He is always on the move, and

simply invites others to follow after him. Those who respond will learn the truth by making the journey. The
word disciple means 'learner', and it is not hard to understand why the New Testament in so many different places
understands a life incorporated into Christ as a journey, a
continual process of learning, an ongoing series of events
that together, step by step and day by day, qualify us not to
be a teacher but to be a learner, to be a disciple, one trained
for the Kingdom of Heaven. This is the story of Paul, con-
verted and taught by the grace of God, set apart to preach
the gospel to the nations.

Life in Christ

What is this gospel? It is 'the power of God for salvation to everyone who has faith, to the Jew first and also
to the Greek' (Romans 1.16). It is the good news that in
Jesus Christ, the God of Israel shows himself faithful to
his covenant of grace, and fulfils the promises made to his
people through the prophets of old. In former times, fellowship with God was the particular privilege of the people of Israel. But now in Jesus God has ushered in the end
time in which all nations will come to worship on the holy
mountain and all people will be drawn into fellowship with
their creator. This gift of salvation is the active love uniting
believers with Christ: we call it the grace of God. 'There
is therefore now no condemnation for those who are in
Christ Jesus' (Romans 8.1).

In Christ, Paul contends, human beings are enabled to
live in a right relationship with their creator, a relationship previously marred by sin and death. God's plan for the
world was not one of disobedience and opposition, but love

in relationship. However, human sin – the nothingness that is human failure to achieve what God wishes for them – has left a void, a gap between creator and created which humans cannot bridge for themselves. That gap is bridged by Christ, and Christ is grace personified. He is the active presence of the divine uniting human beings with himself. In order to traverse the gap we must be united to Christ. Paul describes this being united with the legal metaphor 'justification'. To unpack this word, we need to know just a little Greek. The word we translate 'justification' and the word we translate 'righteousness' have the same root: the Greek equivalents of the letters D I and K. So *dikaiosunē* is usually translated 'righteousness', and *dikaiōma* is usually translated 'justification'. We might expand upon the word 'justification' by suggesting a translation close to 'righteous making' because when he uses the word 'justification' Paul means the gracious act of God whereby sinful human beings are restored to a right relationship with their creator.

That creator, the Lord, the God of Israel, had always lived in relationship with his people – as their maker, their guardian and their redeemer. The God who protects and accompanies the patriarchs is the God who rescues his people from slavery in Egypt so that they may worship him in the land that they have been promised. The God of love seeks out his people to bring them close to him, and the relationship into which he enters with them is a covenant, a coming together, of God and humanity. Despite the infidelity of his people, despite their tendency repeatedly to abandon that covenant relationship, God in his mercy again and again takes the initiative. He restores the covenant relationship by saving his people from the sin and death that separate them from him. In Christ that saving act of God has come

to its final fruition, so that not only the chosen people of
Israel but all of God's children, every created person, Jew
or otherwise, is to be welcomed into the universal covenant
of loving relationship which is defined by the self-giving
love of God.

Grace against the law?

Before we look more closely to see how these ideas play
out in some of Paul's writings, we can help ourselves by
examining a popular but not entirely helpful interpretation
of his ideas that has had a significant place in Christian history. It is an interpretation associated with writings from
the sixteenth-century Reformation and with the idea that
has often been called 'justification by faith'. In fact, when
theologians talk of the doctrine of justification by faith
they ought really to be speaking of the idea of justification by grace through faith, since the act of justification –
of accepting as righteous those who are unrighteous and
restoring them to the covenant relationship of God and his
people – is the act of God himself in his loving kindness,
or grace. Justification entails the twofold aspect of grace
we discussed at the beginning. God in his gracious mercy
justifies the sinner, and grace is both the cause and the consequence of justification. It is the cause because God's free
gift of love accepts us, and it is the consequence because the
love of God enables us to reach beyond ourselves in love.

According to some traditional readings of Paul, grace is
fundamentally opposed to law. The idea here is that the
message of Christ is a specific rejection of a Jewish tradition of legalism. Either we are justified by obeying the
law, or we are justified by the grace of God. On the face

of it there is nothing strange about this reading: after all, Paul himself contrasts 'grace through faith' with 'works of law' repeatedly. 'Works of law' here means 'obedience to the law of Israel', the Torah or instruction by which God's people had tried – and according to Paul failed – to live in relationship with him. We see this contrast drawn sharply in the angry tones of Paul's letter to the Galatians. In this epistle, he upbraids those who, he thinks, are deserting him who called them 'in the grace of Christ' (Galatians 1.6). Their desertion consists in their being persuaded that any Gentile who is welcomed into covenant relationship with God through Christ must undergo the traditional acceptance ritual of circumcision. To insist on this demand, Paul argues, is to insist on full obedience to the law. It is to maintain that a right relationship with God can only be achieved by submission to the Torah and its commands. But acceptance into Christ, Paul is adamant, is the gift of God's grace and cannot be achieved by any human action.

However, while affirming the centrality of grace in Pauline theology (something a book on grace would hardly be expected to contradict!), we might pose a couple of questions. Does Paul's view of grace and justification lead to the rejection of the law? And if so, does this imply that law and grace are in opposition? The reasons for our questioning could be several, and the first of them would be historical. A distinction between Judaism and Christianity in the sense that we understand the terms has no place in the time of Jesus or Paul. It makes no sense of a first-century Jew to suggest that there is something wrong with the law. On the contrary, the law is itself the gift of God's grace. Alone of all the peoples of the world, the nation of Israel has been chosen by God in his gracious mercy for special loving care. This care is manifest in his gift of the law, which enables his people to live in right relationship with him.

Paul's concern is not that the law is thought wrong, but rather that in Christ the end time has come, because Christ is the end of the law, not in the sense of finality, but in the sense of fulfilment. When in Romans 10.4 we read the words 'Christ is the end of the law', that word 'end' is a translation of the Greek word *telos* – end in the sense of goal or fulfilment. Christ is the *telos* of the law, so that everyone who has faith might be justified. Why then the law? To help and guard us, to be our custodian until Christ came, that we might be justified by faith (Galatians 3.24). That word 'custodian' is an interesting one, since it was for a while assumed that the Greek term it translates – *paidagōgos* – was to be understood as a type of schoolmaster, in the ancient world a punitive authority figure who might deal harshly with failure or disobedience. However, the word was used in Paul's time to describe a trustworthy slave whose job it was to see young boys safely to school. That slave was a guardian, keeping the children safe and enabling their education. So the law was the gracious gift of God for the good of his people, a gift that looked towards a future completion (the metaphor here is contrasting childhood with adulthood), at which point no guardian would be needed.

Creation, covenant and Christ

We can begin to see Paul's attitude more clearly if we observe two senses in which he uses the word righteousness and its parallels. That which justifies (makes someone righteous) is that which incorporates us into Christ, that which enables believers to 'get in' to the community of salvation. But the right relationship with God in which believers exist is something ongoing (as was Paul's gradual coming to sight, his learning or discipleship, following his conversion). Here the sense is not 'getting in' but 'staying in', and the commands of the ethical law are God's prescription for good living. Paul's account of his own Jewish existence, which he offers in the letter to the Philippians, makes no suggestion that there was some fundamental problem with Judaism which needed to be overcome. Instead, what he encountered was the grace of God in Christ, not something conforming to expectation but something that exploded previous assumptions with the blinding flash of the Damascus road.

So when Paul writes of believers being made righteous by grace through faith, what does he mean? We can answer this question by following through some of the arguments of the letter to the Romans, which most scholars agree is one of the later of Paul's extant writings. It is a substantial text to which we will not begin to do justice, but even a fairly brief examination will teach us much about grace.

It is often argued that Romans was written for people whom Paul had not yet met. Perhaps it was designed to create possibilities for an expanding Christian mission, expanding beyond Rome to the west of the first-century empire. Certainly Paul is concerned to emphasize that both Jew and Gentile are the recipients of God's gracious love, just as he is concerned to emphasize that all have sinned, and all have fallen short of the glory of God. Jews have failed because they were entrusted with the law but could not obey it; Gentiles have failed because since the foundation of the world the reality of God's power and deity has been shown, and those who failed to honour him are thus without excuse. The distinction between Jew and Gentile has, however, been challenged by the life, death and resurrection of Christ. The true Israel of God is now not a particular people in a particular place, but in those who are united with Christ by baptism. This is not to say that the chosen people had no advantage, or were not the recipients of God's grace through, for example, the gift of the scriptures. But now, since both Jew and Gentile have not lived up to the love of God, and all have fallen short, the righteousness of God has been revealed separately from the old law, even though the law and the prophets bear witness to it. Those who are made righteous, justified, are justified by God's grace in the gift of faith.

As an example, Paul chooses Abraham, the patriarch whose covenant with the God of Israel marks the beginning of God's chosen people and the promises to which Israel looked forward. Scripture – what we call the book of Genesis – says that 'Abraham believed God, and it was reckoned to him as righteousness' (Genesis 15.6, quoted at Romans 4.3). Abraham's faith was displayed in the relationship of hope and trust which he enjoyed with the God who was his creator, the God who brings something from nothing. The gift of God to Abraham and Sarah – the gift of a son beyond their childbearing years – is the creator's gift, because from the absence of life and fertility, from nothing, God brought forth a person – very much something. The characteristic of Abraham is the faith that Paul describes, but of course Abraham, according to scripture, is not simply the father of Isaac but the father of all those who believe, the patriarch of the true Israel. Thus the inherited characteristic of all who belong to this, the chosen family or people of God, is faith in the God whose grace brings something from nothing. Those who are in Christ are those who believe in the same God, the same creator who brings life where there is none: this is the God who raised Jesus from the dead. Therefore, Paul argues, we who believe are justified, made righteous, by faith, the gift of God's grace.

He goes on to consider the contrasting case of Adam. Whereas Abraham hoped in the creative possibilities of God's grace, Adam rejected the right relationship of created to creator by disobeying the command of God in the garden. Thus it was, according to Paul, that through the disobedience of one man sin came into the world, and through sin death. Paul's so-called 'Adam typology' is his demonstration that the ills of the human condition, the sin and death that rule over human beings, are overcome in the new and perfect man, Jesus Christ. Being united to Christ by God's grace, human beings are themselves transformed and not subject to the negative rule of sin.

After Adam and Abraham, the rule of sin was characterized by the law. Does this mean that the law is a bad thing? No. In order to come to terms with Paul's account of the law, especially as it is densely expressed in Romans 7, we need to return to the images of light and dark. Imagine living in complete darkness. One would not be able to see one's situation at all. Being blind to what is really going on, a person might be entirely deluded and think that all was well, when in fact it is not. Shine a light into that darkness, and the reality of one's awful living will become clear. To begin with, however, it will seem as if the light has made things worse (just as did the light that blinded Saul at the 'moment' of his conversion). Illuminating our situation must be a good thing, for it will enable us to identify evil and wrongdoing and seek to overcome them. But our first reaction may well be not to be grateful for the light, but to react to all of the evils it has exposed.

This is Paul's view of God's gift of the law. It enables transgression, if by transgression we mean the specific disobeying of particular commandments. But in fact the commandments that are given are the good gifts of God, because they are the guide to living in a right relationship with God. The law is the brightness that initially alerts us to the squalor of our surroundings, but is then the enabling force that will allow us to tackle that squalor and try to clean up our act.

Sadly, human beings cannot manage that which they claim to desire – behaving well, living in love for God and for one another. It is not the commandment, the law itself, that causes human beings to do wrong. It is the power of sin and evil that uses the opportunity that commandments provide to bring about failure in human lives, failure that is recognized as failure because a commandment has been broken. That which should have been for the good has now become that which indicates our lacks and our nothingness. It allows us to perceive the gap that exists between God's intentions for us – the right living that the law showed the people of Israel – and our own inability to reach the potential with which human beings are created. Knowing our inadequacy we seem trapped by it until the grace of God brings about our rescue through the life, death and resurrection of Christ. Into that life, death and resurrection we are baptized; in Christ we are justified – made righteous – by being those who have received God's gift of faith.

The prophet Habbakuk foresaw a time when the righteous would live by faith (Habakuk 2.4). That time is made present in Christ, and the Kingdom (to use gospel language) is the result. The Kingdom, which is ushered in by the life, death and resurrection of Christ, is that into which all people will be drawn to worship the God of Israel, just as the prophets foretold. In these last days, there is no need for those Gentiles drawn into Christ to be initiated by the physical demands of the law, such as circumcision. Justification for Paul is being upheld as righteous, as if one is the victor in a legal suit, the result of which verdict is membership of the Body of Christ. It is God's grace, God's loving kindness and mercy, by which all people, unworthy as they are, are upheld, made righteous. But this grace that justifies also enables, because the gift of God in showing humans how to live, the gift that is the law, remains holy and just and good.

For Paul, we are united to Christ by baptism. We die to sin, so as to be raised to the new life of Easter, which is Christ's gift to all. In other words, because of God's action in Christ, we receive the grace of God, we are made into something new, we are enabled to live as the Body of Christ. God's grace – his loving mercy – is both the cause of our being accepted and the consequence of that acceptance, because the particular gift of grace in baptism, the gift that originates with the death and resurrection of Christ, makes us into something that we were not before – the adopted children of God.

So Paul's understanding of grace cannot be separated from his understanding of God's love in action, personified in Christ. The God who is creator is the God who enters into covenant with his people. Being justified – living in right relationship with God – is believing in the creator God who brings life from death, in granting a child to Sarah, in raising Jesus from the dead. In his loving action God restores people to that right relationship, welcomes them back into the covenantal love that he has for all his people. Creation, covenant and Christ come together.

The cross of the Son of God

But there is a C we have hardly mentioned in this chapter, and it presses itself urgently upon any examination of Paul and consideration of the love of God. It is the cross of Jesus Christ. In another of his letters, the first letter to the Corinthian church, Paul expresses his anxiety lest anyone in the church orientate his or her thinking with any demonstration, wisdom, rhetoric or authority other than the manifestly unwise love of the crucified Messiah. Some seek miraculous proofs of God's truth, others look for philosophical and intellectual justification, but Paul and his companions preach only Christ crucified (1 Corinthians 1.22f.), which is for some a stumbling block (since the notion of a crucified Messiah confounds those who sought military liberation from an occupying power) and to others folly (for how could the power of God be shown through the death of a common criminal?). Despite his prodigious learning and considerable powers of argument, Paul insists that when he first came to Corinth his resolve was to know nothing except 'Jesus Christ and him crucified' (1 Corinthians 2.2).

In the context of 1 Corinthians, this cruciform field of thought enables Paul to correct and encourage the fledgling church community. But its application for us is wider. There is a danger in our reading of Paul, a danger for us as admirers of his powers of argument and his theological imagination. We might be beguiled into thinking that this talk of creator, covenant and Christ is primarily designed to make sense. We could read Paul as if he were trying to prove a point from first principles, to demonstrate the grace of God as I might demonstrate the validity of a scientific theory or the soundness of a historical argument. But for

Paul and for us, the cross of Christ will always confound such attempts at intellectual demonstration.

'Do you not know that all of us who have been baptized into Christ Jesus were baptized into his death?' asks Paul in Romans 6.3. Paul tells us we are members of the body of Christ, but we could be forgiven for thinking that our incorporation into Christ is akin to joining a club or being part of a society. However, the word 'members' means something deeper. We are members of the Body of Christ because we are organs and limbs of that body – it makes no sense for us to differentiate ourselves from the body. If Christ is a body we are not its fans or supporters, we are his very self, and that union is the union of created and creator that grace brings about, a union made possible and real by the sacrificial love of the Messiah who died on the cross.

Paul refers to the death of Christ in many ways, but repeatedly by employing the language of sacrifice. In Romans 3.25 he describes Christ being put forward by God as a *hilastērion*, a word that is sometimes translated 'expiation', sometimes 'propitiation', sometimes more generally 'atoning sacrifice'. These words take us into the sacrificial world of the Old Testament. When Paul writes that Christ was put to death for our transgressions and raised for our justification, he is employing the contrast of life and death we made earlier. He is also reminding us of the practice of sacrificial offering made as a means of dealing with sin. But sacrifice is more than dealing with sin. Essential to a biblical understanding of sacrifice is the concept of 'offering'. In ancient Israel this idea was played out in lots of ways – in cereal and grain offerings for the harvest, for example; in the offering of the firstborn, which the Gospel of Luke narrates in Jesus' presentation in the Temple (Luke 2.22–38); and in the sin and guilt offerings in which – by presenting to God the most valuable gift of all, the gift of life – the Israelites demonstrate their trust in his mercy to overlook their sins, pass over their transgressions, and continue in his steadfast love.

The offering of perfect life

How can Christians claim that a historical event some two thousand years ago brings about the reconciliation of human and divine? What has the cross of Christ to do with grace? Perhaps we should begin our answer by remembering that the crucifixion is not an event in isolation. We should also remind ourselves of the argument of our previous chapter: the doctrine of grace is rooted in the Christian doctrine of the Trinity. From all eternity God in himself is a perfect community of love. The doctrine of the Trinity tells us that there is nothing of Father, Son and Spirit that is not poured out. This is the true definition of selfless love, because there is literally no self left that is not offered to the other. Human beings are created in the image of God, that is, they are created with the capacity to imitate God, to be like him in love. The purpose of human life is to be divine, to offer a life of perfect love, to God and neighbour. However, human beings, far from being self-less, are fallen and selfish. Unable to grasp what it is to be divine, they snatch at power and pride and authority by keeping for themselves everything that they can. In so doing, they create the individualism, the selfishness, that forbids love and destroys relationships.

However, the will of God is that human beings are united to him in love. Unable to do this for themselves, they are the recipients of God's life of grace through the incarnation. The life of Christ is the life of the Trinity lived out in a human person. There is nothing of Jesus Christ that is not perfectly offered in love to the Father. So it is that Christ's message of unconditional love is matched by his mission of perfect self-giving. For physically limited human beings, and Jesus of Nazareth was one of those, perfect self-giving must be physical as well as spiritual. Jesus must offer his life to the Father, or else he has kept something for himself, he has lived out the selfishness that it is his mission to overcome. The sacrifice of the Son to the Father on the earthly cross of Jesus is thus the worldly story of the life of God himself, the eternal offering of love from Father to Son which is the life of the Trinity. Though a first-century Christian such as Paul would not recognize the technical language of Trinity from later centuries, nevertheless he presents us with a doctrine of grace by which we are united to the life of Christ and baptized into his death and resurrection. The sacrifice of Christ is the offering of humanity, and by grace all who believe are incorporated into that sacrifice.

This mission of the incarnate Son transforms humanity once and for all. Once God has joined humanity to himself, humanity is never the same. It becomes part of the life of God, and since you and I participate in humanity, we are also participants in the divine life, so that when God looks upon us in our sin what he sees is Christ in his love. You and I are 'all at once what Christ is', as the Jesuit poet Gerard Manley Hopkins puts it in echo of the Christian Fathers, since Christ is what we are. But humanity, confronted by the love of God, fears it. Love does not make sense to our power-hungry minds, it threatens our securities and challenges our individualism. The one who incarnates perfect love is thus the one who becomes the enemy of sinful humanity with its pride and its protectiveness. The love of God, personified in Jesus Christ, is thus rejected and condemned, as those who rule seek to do away with the love that threatens them.

Love, however, refuses to conform to our expectations and power structures. The more desperately we try to do away with love, shutting it up in a stone-cold tomb, the more powerfully it bursts forth, mocking our attempts to gain control over that which is truly creative. The perfect humanity of Christ lives for ever in the presence of the Father, so that for all eternity a perfect offering of humanity is being made from Son to Father. This self-giving is itself the grace of God, the perfect love, which God in his mercy shows to all that is created. But because humanity is now transformed, the life, death and resurrection of Christ enable the particular gift of God, which we call grace. This is so because the fact that humanity now lives in the presence of the Father means that human beings can now be so much more than their own abilities allow. God has united his life to ours, so that the life of grace – the life in which we are enabled to enact the love of God – is the life of everyone who is baptized into the death of Christ.

Describing grace and salvation

The grace of God resists our desire for control, but despite that truth we struggle with a determination to explain the cross of Christ and the 'mechanics' of Christian notions of redemption. This aspect of Christian theological talk is usually called 'soteriology', the study of salvation. Such study cannot and should not be separated from Christology, from Christian teaching about the person and nature of Jesus Christ. It is worth pausing at this point and remarking that the language of justification which so concerned us in Paul is metaphorical language. It is talk of something (the loving acts of God) in terms of something else (ancient legal practice). We need to be careful here. We are mistaken if we think that the relationship between God's love and grace, and the death and resurrection of Jesus, is akin to a series of transactions or causes and effects, by which grace may be somehow 'released'.

Instead, we should remember that grace is the basis of all our talk of redemption. Christian theology does not begin with an intellectual problem – the problem of sin and alienation from God – and calculate a solution – the grace of God in Jesus Christ. Rather, the solution precedes the problem (as is sometimes said of Paul's attitude to the law). Grace is central to the ways in which Christians tell the story of God's love; it is not something that is discovered as the denouement of those stories. Grace is not the treasure we are looking for, it is the map that guides us. Some challenge traditional Christian understandings of salvation by asking, 'Why could God not simply forgive'? Why, for example, should we offer an account of God's action that appeals to images of satisfying divine honour, or defeating the powers of sin and death, or rescuing human beings from the fate of eternal darkness? Why couldn't God simply forgive?

The Christian doctrine of grace gives the answer 'he has'. Salvation presupposes grace, and Christian theology presupposes salvation. Those writers and thinkers in the past who have sought to find new and fitting ways to describe the act of God in reconciling humanity to himself – Paul included – are writers who have presupposed the grace of God. They have taken for granted the reality of transformed human life, transformed because humanity is united to the divine offering of Son to Father.

We can try to get to grips with these rather puzzling theological arguments by looking at the work of the eleventh- and twelfth-century monk and archbishop, Anselm of Canterbury, whose dialogue *Cur Deus Homo* (*Why God became Man*) is often condemned as the coldest and most transactional of all salvation stories. In it Anselm demonstrates that while it was fitting and necessary that humanity should be restored to relationship with God, it was also the case that only God could effect that restoration. Thus the incarnation, death and resurrection of Christ are the story of the satisfaction made by the incarnate Christ, the price of restoration paid in order to save human beings from the punishment for sin which was their due. We may or may not like such an approach (and we certainly have not done justice to it in that summary), but the purpose of raising it is to point to something else. Early on in his dialogue Anselm tells his imaginary interlocutor (the amusingly named Boso) that he is attempting a new narrative of salvation because he is fed up by the inadequacy of other ways of telling the story. Those ways are compared with the efforts of bad painters who in trying to represent Christ succeed only in depicting the Lord of all as ugly (Anselm, *Why God became Man*, I.1).

This comparison is striking. Anselm is calling to mind the portrayal of Christ perhaps in the decoration of a church or on a particular wall or panel. Such portrayals are not attempts at imitation, as if the artist knew exactly what the historical Jesus of Nazareth looked like and was trying to reproduce that precise image. It is a matter of history that the real person Jesus lived, died and had a particular appearance, one that doubtless changed over time as do we all. But the person who dares to paint him does not claim to recall that appearance. Instead he or she attempts to interpret the person being painted without copying any literal or visual original. Now compare this with talking about grace and salvation. Anselm's attempts at describing God's act of love in Christ are not efforts to replicate something, or to paint by numbers from a prototype so that there is a precise match in which we can rejoice. Rather, they are efforts at offering an account or a story of a truth beyond our understanding. As the great Austrian philosopher Wittgenstein said of language, we can describe but not explain or give foundation (Wittgenstein, *Philosophical Investigations*, p. 49).

Grace is central to our description. How is it that we are where we are, how can it be that human beings are united to the life of God? The answer is grace. It is not an answer that we deduce by deliberation, but an answer that is presupposed in all that Christians teach. Our human life and destiny is crossed, contradicted and embraced, by the grace of God that transforms what it means to be human. Paul's every understanding and expectation was crossed by the grace of God that drew him into Christ. Living in Christ, he opened for the early Christian communities new ways of describing the love of the creator God who is faithful to his covenant and enables that covenant relationship with all peoples in the life, death and resurrection of Christ into which people are baptized. The basis for this thinking was, and had to be, the folly of God's grace in the cross of Jesus Christ.

5

Grace and human being(s)

See how these Christians love one another

The early Christian writer Tertullian reports a number of remarks made concerning Christians by some of those whom we now call pagans. One of his reports goes like this: '"Look", they say, "how they love one another" (for they themselves hate one another) "and how they are ready to die for one another"' (Tertullian, *Apology*, 39.7). In popular paraphrase this saying has come down to us as 'See how these Christians love one another', but sadly, and all too often, those words are used in sarcasm. Many Christians have been, and are, good at loving one another, but too many Christians have been too good at failing to fulfil the new commandment that Jesus gives in John 13, to 'love one another as I have loved you'. The theological disputes that litter Christian history give us plenty of examples of such failings.

The British theologian Pelagius is one of those whom Christian history has named a heretic. (Though this word has become a bogey term, it initially just meant a member of a sect or party.) Pelagius and others were involved in what became a long-running theological dispute with the great North African bishop Augustine of Hippo (354–430) at the beginning of the fifth century, and it is a dispute that has resurfaced in many forms at many times in Christian history. Unhappily for what should be a happy subject, it is a dispute about grace and – in particular – about the relationship between divine and human action. Are human beings given the gift of freedom? And is this freedom affected by the outpouring of love which is the grace of God? If so, how? If grace unites me to Christ and to the life of the Trinity, am I still choosing, acting, loving, failing to love? Can grace threaten my ability to choose my own course? Can my freedom, without the help of God's grace, be of any aid to my attempts to love? These are the questions that concern us in this chapter and the next.

The course of the 'Pelagian controversy' is a fascinating aspect of early Christian history but its detail is beyond our scope. The arguments continued long after Pelagius had disappeared from the scene, his fate rather unclear. To begin with, Pelagius was a teacher of some influence in early fifth-century Rome who, along with many (Christian and otherwise) reacted forcefully against what he saw as the indulgence of late Roman society. The tendency of some in their affluent circumstances to enjoy excessive drinking, gambling, adultery, gluttony and the like offended the zealous Pelagius, an ascetic Christian concerned to live according to scripture and to obey the commands of Jesus in the Gospels and of Paul in his Epistles. This was a bad time to be in Rome – the city would be sacked by Alaric the Goth in 410. Pelagius seems to have left the western capital before this cataclysmic event, which many saw as a judgement on precisely the moral disorder to which he and his followers objected. The ideas that Augustine and others associate with Pelagius were propagated, it appears, largely by one particular follower, Celestius, and by the year 412 Augustine was sufficiently exercised by the dispute to write a number of theological treatises which have come to be known as 'anti-Pelagian'.

'See how these Christians love one another.' The ironic use of that phrase applies to the Pelagian controversy partly because much of what Augustine opposed was not directly taught by Pelagius himself. Nevertheless, it is he who has become the 'heresiarch' (arch heretic), a baddie of Christian theology. The main lines of argument can be sketched. Pelagius, it is said, had come across Augustine's celebrated spiritual and intellectual autobiography, the *Confessions*, and had not liked everything he saw. He objected in particular to what he took to be Augustine's downplaying of human responsibility and freedom to act well or badly. 'Give what you command, and command what you will', Augustine had written (*Confessions* X, 29). This puzzled Pelagius. If human beings are not able to act well, then the moral imperative to obey the commands of scripture seemed obsolete.

Loyalty to scripture

Pelagius' basic argument seems straightforward. Any reader of the scriptures finds that much is demanded of the Christian. It is surely reasonable to insist that the teaching of Jesus in the Sermon on the Mount, for example, is not just something to which Christians can aspire but something they can actually attain. After all, if I am incapable of doing a particular thing, Christ would not tell me to do it. Jesus gives commands, and hence the commands of Jesus can be obeyed. These assumptions are simple, but underneath them are further assumptions concerning the nature of sin. Pelagius and his followers were right to observe that the word sin is used in the Bible in many different ways. They were also emphatic in their objection to the notion that sin was something real, a substance that acted upon human nature. Were that the case, then creation would not be something that was genuinely good, but rather a dualistic realm of light and dark. Such a view does not seem to fit into the understanding of all that was made which Christians learned from the book of Genesis. (Augustine agreed, as we shall see.) Augustine reports Pelagius as asking whether a specific sin can be avoided or not: if the latter, then it is not sin; if the former, it is possible for human beings to live without sin, since sin can be avoided.

Augustine did not do justice to Pelagius, or to the later and fiercer opponents who persisted with and developed their arguments long after 'Pelagianism' had been condemned in the year 418. However, we should be wary of romanticizing the so-called heretic simply because he has been misreported. Augustine's understanding of grace and human freedom came to dominate Christian discussions of the subject not because people had been tricked into misreading his opponents, but because of the extraordinary power and insight of his own ideas.

Simply put, if Pelagius is concerned that Augustine's ideas lead to an abrogation of human moral responsibility, then Augustine is equally concerned that Pelagius' teaching denigrates the grace of God. Several issues are at stake: what do we mean by freedom? Why is moral failure characteristic of humans, and, perhaps most importantly, what are the implications for our understanding of human choice of the assertion that God is the creator of all things?

Who or what is free?

Early in his career, Augustine had written on the subject of human choice, and had done so partly to oppose his own past. His target was Manichean dualism: the Manichees (named after the third-century Iranian prophet Mani) maintained that people made evil choices because their physical nature was fundamentally evil. The young Augustine had been deeply influenced by these ideas. In opposing his former view, the mature Augustine defended the freedom of choice human beings have. Sin is not a substance, but a result of the exercise of the will (a view Pelagius also held, as we have seen).

Sin, however, does not have a cause, because sin is defined by a negative (by choosing that which is not the will of God). Augustine's point here is that evil is not a thing but an absence of something – a 'privation of good', as he argues in his slightly later *Confessions* – and it is a contention that has proved hugely important in Christian theology. The doctrine of creation is at its heart. God is the creator of all, and scripture tells us that God saw all that he had made, and it was very good. God, who is nothing other than perfect self-giving love, is the definition of goodness. That which is evil, or sinful, is defined as such not by being anything in particular – not like this or like that – but by being contrary to something else. We describe something as evil because it lacks the goodness that is God's love. So that which we call sin and evil is, in that strict sense, not something that exists. I alluded to this view in Chapter 1, when raising the issue of the gap that exists between human potential and human achievement. It is this gap, this absence, that we call sin. But we should recall the danger of words: to say it does not, in a strict sense, exist is not to deny its danger. Holes, gaps, chasms are, or should be, worrying. But they are defined by not being something else. As the great Dominican teacher Herbert McCabe used to say, 'if you inadvertently drive your car over a cliff you will have nothing to worry about; it is precisely the nothing that you will have to worry about' (McCabe, *God Matters*, p. 29).

Augustine completed his treatise on free choice seven years after beginning it, and his thinking seems to have developed. Towards its end, he argues that freedom of the will is an 'intermediate good', because it can be used either foolishly or wisely (Augustine, *On Free Choice of the Will*, 3, 18, 52). This idea follows from an assumption common to his thought world (and many such afterwards), that what we mean by 'will' is very closely related to what we mean by 'intellect' or 'understanding'. To will or to want something is to understand it to be good from my point of view. If I consider money to be beneficial for me, I recognize it to be a good, and so I want it. Augustine's observations of human nature led him to conclude that human beings are not equally capable, on their own, of using this 'intermediate good' well or badly. Rather, they are inclined most of the time to make the wrong choices.

This view of Augustine's has been seen by some as an unfairly pessimistic view of human nature. We will consider shortly how far this is the case. It is undoubtedly a view that colours his subsequent thought on grace and human action. When he wrote to his bishop in Milan on the subject, years before he had heard of Pelagius, he was already convinced that he had understood why it was that human beings were condemned to fail in their efforts to be good. Human beings were born sinful, they had inherited from the first human being – Adam – both the tendency to sin, which left them helpless, and the guilt of that first sin, which left them liable to punishment. This original sin has corrupted the human will so that, far from being able to decide on equal terms between that which is Godly and that which is evil, human beings are biased towards the absence of good. All that could assist them was the grace, the free gift, of God.

The necessity of grace

It would be wrong then to argue that the Pelagian controversy made Augustine any more gloomy about the corruption of the human will than he already was. It is worth remembering that he considered himself a true interpreter of St Paul. The letter to his bishop Simplician takes as its basis Paul's questioning of the Corinthian church: have they any grounds on which to boast? No, because all is the gift of God's grace. 'For who sees anything different in you? What do you have that you did not receive? And if you received it, why do you boast as if it were not a gift?' (1 Corinthians 4.7). Pelagius too saw himself as properly Pauline (Christian theological disputes are rarely about philosophy and usually about the Bible). But Pelagius maintained that the transformation brought about by God's acceptance of the believer by grace meant that a new human being was born, one who could live up to the demands of the gospel, one who could strive along with Paul for the perfection of Christ.

Augustine's so-called 'anti-Pelagian writings' demonstrate his understanding that the human will is damaged by the sin of Adam. His earlier writings suggested that the will might be seen as a 'middle good', equally capable of being used well or badly. This, he feels, will no longer do. The danger is that such a view might be taken to imply that human beings can, of themselves, make something good (an action of the will). If they can do this apart from the grace of God, then they seem to add goodness to that which God has made. The idea Augustine wants to avoid is this: God makes the human capacity to choose and human beings can choose to do well, thus creating goodness that wasn't there.

Although his ideas may seem complex, Augustine's first concern here is not philosophical abstraction about the nature of the human will. What dominates his thinking is the reality of human sin. It is no surprise, then, to find him reading and expounding St Paul as the basis for his insistence that obeying commandments cannot be the source of human justification before God. Romans 7, which we examined earlier, is never far away: 'I do not do the good I want, but the evil I do not want is what I do' (Romans 7.19). Just as the law cannot justify, so the will cannot save. What, then, of freedom? It cannot be opposed to grace, because freedom is the gift of God himself. Freedom is, in other words, the result of grace and not its opponent. It is not the capacity to choose that defines freedom. What makes human beings reflect most fully the image of God in which they were created is the capacity to align one's will with the love of God. To be truly free is to live in that image that is restored in us by the grace of baptism, by which we are united to Christ.

Quoting the passage in John's Gospel, 'I am the vine, you are the branches', Augustine reminds his readers that Jesus himself says, 'apart from me, you can do nothing' (John 15.5; Augustine, *Homilies on the Gospel of John* 81). It is the grace of God that enables humanity both to will and to act. Here we see being developed the twofold understanding of grace that was set out in our first chapter: the good Christians do is the fruit of faith, and is hence the gift of God to the believer. The grace of God is co-operative, in that God takes the initiative, bringing it about that human beings have the will to do good, and then works with those human beings who have that will, to bring good its completion. Augustine quotes Philippians 2.13, 'it is God who is at work in you, enabling you both to will and to work for his good pleasure', to make this point (Augustine, *On Grace and Free Will* 21, in *Anti-Pelagian Writings*).

Sin (originally)

Much debate in the controversy that followed centred upon the baptism of infants, its necessity or otherwise. Such a demand follows from the claim that all people inherit the guilt of Adam through the physical process of human reproduction. Few ideas have had a more notorious legacy in the Church and western society generally, but it is easy to dismiss an ancient thinker without taking him seriously. It is true that Augustine locates in physical desire the strongest example of the human tendency to make choices that conflict with the will of God. It often amuses students to discover that, when speculating as to the state of the first man and woman before they fell by disobeying God, Augustine suggested that the man would have been in complete rational control of his reproductive faculties. Making the decision to make love, he could 'switch on' his physical prowess by choice. But Augustine deserves more credit than giggling, because he knows human beings better than we might like to admit. A man's inability to exercise control over his sexual desire is not, for Augustine, constitutive of human sin. Rather, it is a demonstration, a symptom, of the corruption of the will.

Imagine not being able to control your right arm; it would be a strange and debilitating state of affairs (and is for those people who suffer from just such a condition). That which clouds our judgement – we might use the example of alcohol rather than lust – sees us make choices, sees us want things that, ordinarily and rationally, we know to be folly. I can (probably wrongly) come to the conclusion that drinking several units of alcohol would be good for me, because I would enjoy it, and thus I would want to consume said drink. However, the influence of the drink will actually harm me in that it will further impair my ability sensibly to choose. In such cases, the desires of self overwhelm our better understanding of what is good, and our choices serve only to do that which we think will help ourselves (but, as with too much alcohol, which actually do us harm). In so doing, all too often, they also harm others. This is the reality of human life with which Augustine is concerned.

That is all very well, we might say, but Augustine interprets the book of Genesis in a way that is foreign to most Christians today. Rather than reading the creation stories which begin that book as chronicles or historical records of events that are held to be facts, we are comfortable with the notion that biblical narratives are concerned not with historical facts but with truth of a different sort, and that the tales and images with which we are presented are representative of a theological perspective. In Genesis we are being taught that God is the creator of all; that all that God creates is good; that human beings were created in the image of God with a unique place in creation; and that human beings have failed to live up to that image. If there was no historical Adam, there was no historical fall, and if there was no historical fall, there cannot be any literal seminal transmission of inherited guilt and original sin from one generation to another.

'Original sin' is a doctrine that is not helped by its name. When we use the words we think too quickly of chronology – of the very first human beings. Modern scientific understanding prevents us from making such a simple identification. But it remains hard to examine human beings, historical or contemporary, and conclude that all is well. However it has understood its origin, Christian theology has struggled with the reality of humanity. It is a reality that fails to love and to give, that fails, in other words, to imitate Christ and enact the image of God that is its potential.

We shall say more about that image in the next chapter, but in concluding this one we need to revert to our definition of sin. When Augustine identifies evil as a privation of good, he is doing something thoroughly scriptural. The New Testament's word for sin is the word *hamartia*, a Greek word that literally means 'missing the target'. It has its origins in archery. From the earliest Christian writings, then, our notion of sin has been that which is defined not by a positive but by a negative, by a failure to achieve, not an achievement itself. Human beings can choose the way of God. They can choose to be loving, generous, selfless, giving. When so doing, they are not properly called 'sinful'. But human beings can, and do, tend to choose self over others. There is something about us that, on the one hand, so often fails to be loving, and, on the other hand, recognizes our potential to do far better than we actually manage. The gap between those two is what we call 'sin', and it is 'original' in the sense that it is part of us, whether we like it or not. Humanity left to itself has an ugly history, a history of ever more advanced methods of promoting self and destroying others. Humanity needs the grace of God.

6

Creation, grace and human freedom

God the creator

Few people would deny that human beings are in some sense free. Augustine certainly did not. He argued that the freedom to choose is a God-given gift in creation. Had human beings not fallen away from the image of God, that gift would have been exercised for the good. For other thinkers, however, human free will had to be seen as entirely separate from God's creative act. Human freedom can seem to provide defenders of God with an 'excuse' on behalf of the Almighty: the world doesn't work as well as it ought, but that is entirely because of human freedom, which has nothing to do with God. If human freedom is absolute then grace must either destroy human freedom or not affect the choice of human beings. Either way, Augustine's opponents – in his lifetime and today – would have been able to convict him of error. He cannot, they crow, have it both ways.

Augustine and the Christian tradition disagree with this attitude not because of biblical teaching about grace so much as biblical teaching about creation (teaching which, as we have seen, underlies the understanding of grace we find in the New Testament). God is the creator of everything. Everything. Not simply the things we like, but everything that exists. That is why evil does not 'exist' for Augustine. Evil is defined as that which is contrary to God, therefore it cannot have been created by God, therefore it cannot in the strict sense 'exist'. It is an absence, a negative, a lack of something. That is why sin means 'missing the target' – it is sin that misses the mark of human potential. But if God truly is the creator of everything, should we not be troubled by our assumptions concerning human freedom? Most of us tend to assume that in order to be free, human beings must be unconstrained by anything else, unaffected decisively by any power external to themselves. If they are subject to force from another agent, they are not free, and they are not responsible. However, Augustine and those after him make a further and different assumption. If my free action is nothing whatsoever to do with God, then it cannot be the case that God is truly the creator of everything. Why? Because there exists something in the universe that is not created by God – and that thing is my free action. If God is truly creator, then my free choice is just as much created by him as the birds of the air and the fish of the sea. God cannot be absent from my action, for anything from which God is absent is a thing which does not exist.

Now, you may object that this understanding of creation nullifies human freedom entirely. But I suggest that such an objection is labouring under another mistaken assumption, the assumption that God is an agent in the created order. Human freedom could be constrained when human beings are acted upon by other agents (if they are forced by other agents to act in a particular way). But God is not another agent in creation. Rather, God is that which makes freedom possible in the first place through creation. True freedom is the gift of God, and God is – among other descriptions – that without which no freedom is possible. It cannot, therefore, be sensible to oppose divine and human action, as if both these terms refer to things within our ken, within the universe.

Some have found difficulty with this approach. Is such an appeal to the 'otherness' of God, the 'ineffability' (that which cannot be said) of the divine, anything more than a cop-out? Certainly. I suggest – as Augustine does in the *Confessions* – that it is a necessary consequence of speaking of God as creator. When we do talk in this way, we can be misled by the fact that there are lots of different words we can use to refer to God as creator. We might speak of God making the heavens and the earth, or forming the world, or shaping the skies. If we do, we should note the partial nature of our language, because creation – in its theological sense – properly means 'bringing something from nothing'. Essential to Augustine's notion of God is the Bible's teaching that only the love of God is truly creative, only the love of God – God himself – brings something from nothing. Talk of genuine 'nothing' is, however, itself necessarily limited. I cannot conceive of 'nothing', only of things and then the absence of things. But the absence of anything is beyond my comprehension.

There is a further point to be made. When I speak of creation, I am not speaking of a thing, a phenomenon, with which I can compare other things. The creative act of God is not a literal 'making' or 'forming' or 'shaping'. All three of those verbs assume that I start with something and make it into something else. The creative act of God, however, is the eternal act of God's love – God's pouring out of his own Trinitarian life – which is the reason that there is something rather than nothing. We should notice here that this is not an *explanation* of the world. In order to explain the world, to give reasons for it, I must have points of comparison, other possibilities, a series of alternatives that it makes sense to weigh up and hold against one another. But the act of creation will not fall into any such categories. With what can I compare everything?

For these reasons we can see why it is often misleading when theologians talk about 'science and creation', because science – the efforts of human understanding to describe the nature of the universe – is not to be compared or contrasted with creation, but is rather part of it. (Creation is everything there is, and everything there is exists, as Julian of Norwich famously observed, because of God's love.) But we can also see why the temptation to align or oppose grace and human freedom is so great, because our desire to understand is never far from our desire to control, to pin something down, and we will only pin God down if we are not, in fact, dealing with God, but rather with a projection of the divine that fits within our understanding of the created order. So we must resist attempts to assume we can define God, describe divinity as being like this rather than like that, or here rather than there, or now rather than then. Instead we speak the language of human limitation, the language that God hallows by speaking his word in Jesus Christ.

Grace and divine action

These ideas should help us understand that grace is not opposed to human freedom. Why? Because God is not an individual agent opposed to another similar individual agent (you or me). But how then are we going to talk about God acting? As with all our theological language, we do so from within, not attempting to step conceptually outside the

created order. The Bible and the Christian tradition talk of
God acting because things happen that God brings about.
When and where do things happen? At particular times
and in particular places. And thus we locate the action of
God. We don't suggest that God is limited by those loca-
tions or identifications, they simply allow us to articulate
our claims about the creative love of God. When we say
that God parted the waters for the Israelites to cross and
escape the armies of Egypt, we can say that this event happened in a place (though – inevitably – biblical scholars
argue about which one!). But we don't mean that God was
in that place when the event happened, as I would have to
be in my garden in order to cut my lawn. Talking of God's
actions, and assuming that God is the same as we are, are
two quite different things.

A useful way of thinking about these questions can be
found in the writings of medieval theologians, many of
whom found it helpful to borrow and transform the ideas
of the great philosopher Aristotle (BC 384–322). He con-
siders the relationship between things or people who act
(we will call them 'agents'), and the things and people
on whom they act (we will call them 'patients'). He argues that the action of the agent is located in the patient,
in the thing or person being acted upon. What does this
mean? An illustration will help. Aristotle likes the example
of a teacher and a pupil. The former can stand in front
of a blackboard or a PowerPoint display, use every kind of
clever word and exhibit a rare talent for explaining difficult
concepts. But if nobody is listening – if, for example, the
students are all reading messages on their iPhones – then the
teacher is not actually teaching. He or she is simply speaking. In order for there to be teaching happening, somebody
has to be learning. So although the teacher might perform

exactly the same action in two opposite cases – one where the students are attending and one where they are messing about with technology – only one of these is properly described as teaching because the definition of the action ('teaching') depends on something we identify in those being acted upon ('learning').

We can use this distinction to talk about the times of actions as well as their descriptions. If I kick a football towards a goal, some time will pass between my foot touching the ball and the ball crossing the line and entering the net. The goal is scored when, and only when, the ball crosses the line. But my 'action' in scoring the goal has already involved all the physical movement it is going to involve. When did I score the goal? When the ball crossed the line, not when I swung my foot. (Moral philosophers have found it interesting to apply these ideas to action we might wish to condemn: if I poison a reservoir and people subsequently die, when did I kill them?)

The action of God the creator can be articulated in just such a way. It is simply impossible for me to locate and identify the act of creating, of bringing something from nothing. Instead, I take for granted the existence of the created order (I make the assumption, uncontroversial to all but a few radical sceptics, that some things exist) and within that framework I talk of divine activity. Thus I can answer questions such as 'When did God raise Jesus Christ from the dead?', even though the act of God, as Augustine would remind us, is eternal. There is 'a time and a place' for God's actions, because time and place are part of God's creation, and through that creation we speak of God the creator.

Grace, the outpouring of God's love to unite our lives with his, can be 'identified' in such worldly terms: first of all in the historical individual Jesus of Nazareth, and subsequently in all events that we acknowledge as part of our Christian experience. The act of believing in Christ is the result of the grace of God in the gift of faith. Acknowledging God as creator is responding to the grace of God in all that has been made. These actions are unequivocally my actions, freely performed by me because they are not constrained or coerced by anything else. But, since God is the creator of all things, it is also true that they depend on God. Were it not for the creative act of God that is sustaining everything at every moment of its existence, there would be no freedom and no action at all.

So perhaps Augustine's understanding of grace and freedom that we encountered in the last chapter might have more to commend it than modernity has tended to think. However, we would be naive if we thought it an understanding that Christians have always favoured. From the fifth century, we must jump forward more than a thousand years and think about another, even greater, Christian dispute: the conflicts and ruptures that we call the European Reformation. If it is only by the grace of God that I can be saved, there seems little I can do to remedy my human situation. I can trust in God, and nothing else. When I die, so the argument presumably goes, my fate is determined by whether or not I have received that grace.

Reforming an old debate

However, what if other possibilities were open to me? The Western Church in the Middle Ages, unhappy at the notion that anyone might be in a fit state to be admitted to the presence of God at the end of their human lives, taught that people needed to undergo a period of cleansing, or purging, so that their sins could be washed away. This purgatory was not something eternal, but involved a painful process of purification that no one would wish upon any loved one for longer than was absolutely necessary. Thus the system of indulgences came to be born, the idea that the Western Church – most obviously in the person of the Pope of Rome – had the authority to pronounce upon the time souls spent in purgatory. To minimize the length of time one's loved ones underwent painful purgation, one could do things to earn them credit. In particular, one could buy the 'indulgence' of the Church as a sort of 'get out of jail' card (not 'free', of course).

This system of 'indulgences' was one of the principal sources of controversy when, at the beginning of the sixteenth century, the thought of Augustine was revived and reinterpreted, most famously by the German monk Martin Luther. His teaching duties at the University of Wittenberg had seen him study closely Augustine's writings on the Psalms and on Romans, and his emphasis on Augustine's theology of grace eventually led to his own theological breakthrough, which has gone down in theological history as his 'tower experience' (the terminology, from his own reminiscences years later, has been amusingly misunderstood as implying that the experience took place while he was on a monastic loo!). Luther maintained that the 'righteousness of God,' of which Paul writes so powerfully, is a gift not a characteristic. That is to say, the righteousness of God is the righteousness from God, that which God gives to each sinful human being who is the recipient of grace. Luther – reading and writing in Latin – reads the word 'righteousness' as *iustitia*, and so the free gift of God's grace is justification. In Luther's reading, the objection Paul offers to any who require Gentiles to submit to the Jewish law in order to be incorporated into Christ, becomes a polemic against those in the Christian Church who appear to require believers to do particular things (such as purchasing indulgences) in order to receive the grace of God.

Although Luther's theology of grace is thoroughly Augustinian, its expression and emphasis made it the dominant idea of the Christian revolution that we call the Reformation. The young German university teacher came later to symbolize the struggle of the individual believer against the might of ecclesiastical power. Luther's gospel of grace placed each believer in a position of equal standing under the judgement of God and his mercy, and stressed both the absolute freedom of every Christian and that Christian's obligation to imitate Christ and serve others. The contradictory or cruciform aspect of grace that we have stressed is well exemplified in Luther's celebrated 'theology of the cross', another facet of his reading of St Paul. He condemns prevailing theological attitudes by contrasting the theologian of glory, who looks for God in triumph and splendour, with the true theologian who – like Moses in the cleft of the rock in Exodus 33 – catches only a glimpse of God from behind in the suffering and agony of the cross. The God who is revealed is, paradoxically, the hidden God, the one who demonstrates not his power and strength but his infinite mercy and love in offering himself for humanity. The stress upon grace and justification as the gift of God which humans are powerless to earn is a similar contradiction – in Luther's eyes – of that which the Church appeared to be teaching with its theology of indulgences and 'merit'.

The merits of salvation

That last word, 'merit', demands some attention. To some extent, we can characterize Luther's conflict with the European church of his time along the lines of a seeming conflict between the writings of Paul (especially Romans and Galatians) and the less well-known letter of James, the New Testament document in which we find the words:

> What good is it, my brothers and sisters, if you say you have faith but do not have works? Can faith save you? If a brother or sister is naked and lacks daily food, and one of you says to them, 'Go in peace; keep warm and eat your fill', and yet you do not supply their bodily needs, what is the good of that? So faith by itself, if it has no works, is dead. (James 2.14–17)

The issue seems straightforward. If justification is by faith alone, what place have the good deeds enjoined upon Christians in the scriptures? This is, in slightly different form, the question of the Pelagian controversy. Those who had argued that human beings should do that which was within them in order for God to make them righteous were attracted to the language of 'merit', whereby humans could, by performing acts of love and obedience, build up for themselves a store of grace that would count in their favour before the judgement throne of God. This idea, as we have seen, would have horrified Augustine, just as it did Luther and his Augustinian understanding of grace: the free gift of God's sovereignty to believers, who are unable of themselves to do anything to help themselves. The term Pelagian has – unjustly for Pelagius – come to mean the view that I or others can somehow earn grace or salvation by performing particular actions of my own free choice.

However, we should be cautious about rejecting 'merit' entirely. First of all, all human beings are the recipients of 'merit' because all humanity is transformed by the incarnation. As we saw in the last chapter, the offering of Christ upon the cross is the offering of humanity itself, not simply the offering of an individual. Its benefits – union with God – are the gifts of God's grace for all. Second, human actions are not isolated events that bear no relation to one another. Being drawn by God to participate in the divine life involves, among other things, being taught by the Spirit what it means to be a Christian. Living out that Christian life entails doing different things or, as Aquinas might put it, practising Christian virtue. And virtue is not something I possess the way I possess a car, it is something I do, something that becomes a habit because I put it into practice. Living well, putting God and others first, trying to love and live generously, is a continuous process of trial and error at which I can become better, and I become better by doing things over and over again. This, then, is the true 'merit' that God grants human beings – the ability to live in accordance with his love. This is not an ability that is earned, nor one that should in any way be thought of as separate from the grace of God. Rather, it is itself the gift of grace – merit does not earn us grace, rather grace provides us with merit. Grace, personified by Christ and experienced by human beings, is thoroughly practical, as we shall see in the next chapter.

But the sovereignty of God's grace raises another problem, one from which Augustine and his later adherents did not shy away. If believers are believers because of the grace of God, does that not mean that the receipt of grace is eternally chosen by God for us, that we are 'predestined' or 'elected' to the unity with Christ which is salvation? Many in the sixteenth century thought so, and we associate that view most strongly with one of the most famous of Augustinian thinkers, John Calvin (1509–64). No book on grace can avoid mention of Calvin, and before we think any more about predestination we should note a couple of things. First of all, the idea that predestination is a particularly Protestant view of Christianity is – historically – rather strange. There is little real difference between Calvin's basic teaching on the subject and that of Thomas Aquinas, for example. Second, as is true with many who give their names to 'isms', Calvin was not a 'Calvinist', and some of the disputes concerning grace that occurred later result from particular interpretations of his work, interpretations that we may or may not find congenial.

Calvin was primarily a student of scripture, as was Augustine, and both recognized predestination to be a scriptural notion. Paul refers to those whom God foreknew, and predestined, in Romans for example (Romans 8.29). In many ways predestination is just a consequence of a doctrine of providence, the Christian teaching that history is in the loving care of God, that events work themselves out throughout the entire course of the world's long story as part of the divine plan. But, as we observed above, the 'effects' of God's creation are identified because we can identify changes in the world, not because God is acting temporally or changing his mind. Providence and creation cannot properly be separated. Just as predestination is an aspect of providence so providence is an aspect of creation: everything that exists only exists because it is being created – brought from nothing – by the love of God at every moment of that existence. Theologians sometimes talk of 'continuous creation': providence is another expression of the same thing.

because God is not an agent external to an acting human subject. God is not outside us, against us, before us or after us. Rather we are part of the creative possibilities that are God's. Second, as I hinted above, we can hesitate at the temporal force contained in the idea that God acts 'before' us. Again, we are afraid of compromising freedom because when agents coerce other agents there is a temporal priority in their action. But God's action is only temporal because, as we have seen, we identify God's actions by their effects not by any change in God, as if God acts on a whim. And third, and most importantly, by returning to the subject of Chapter 2, the basis of the doctrine of grace in the Christian teaching that God is Father, Son and Holy Spirit.

Protestant theology found it helpful to develop Calvin's teaching by considering what it means to be chosen, 'elected' by God. The most significant of recent Protestant thinkers, the Swiss theologian Karl Barth, reworked a Calvinist notion of predestination in his Christology. Calvin is often associated with the notion of 'double predestination', a seemingly harsh view of grace since not only are some predestined to receive it, some are predestined not to receive it, and hence are predestined not to be saved. (We might observe that all Calvin is doing here is being consistent: those who speak of predestination to grace usually also insist on the necessity of grace for salvation – in that sense, predestination is 'double', an either/or not a both/and.) Barth maintains that in Jesus Christ God has elected humanity to salvation and also that, in the self-giving of the incarnation, God has predestined himself to the condemnation and death that he suffers as a man. Predestination is 'double' for God, and God is doubly the subject and object of predestination because Jesus Christ is both the God who elects and the human being who is elected.

7

Ways of thinking about grace

As we saw in the previous chapter, grace has been a source of controversy in Christian history. Sometimes this controversy has been part of much wider divisions, such as those that characterize the Protestant Reformation in the sixteenth century; sometimes, however, disputes about grace have had a content that we today might call more 'academic'. We need to be wary of using that terminology in a derogatory way. Modern thinking often seems to struggle with the intellectual giants of the Christian past. I think much of that struggle, however, stems from an assumption that the intellectual life is something divorced from practice. In a Christian context, this would mean divorced from a worshipping and praying community. But Christian theology, properly practised, can never be separated from Christian life. Grace, as a subject of theological discussion, is always secondary in Christian theology to grace itself: the reality of God acting in the life of the Church and hence of individual Christians.

In Chapter 4 we saw that theological reflection on the saving act of God – sometimes called soteriology – was unlikely to be helpful if it set about trying to explain the loving act of God. It is too easy to try to pin God down into a story with a beginning, middle and end. That story would probably examine humanity first, come to some conclusions about its problems, and then define a version of salvation that answers all our requirements. The medieval theologian Anselm was offered as an example of someone who is often wrongly read in this way. Anselm, in fact, presupposes the grace of God, and hence the saving acts of God, in all that he writes. Theology should not be a speculative process of reason that leads us from ourselves to conclusions about the God of Jesus Christ. Rather, it is the reflection of the Christian community upon the life it claims to live: life in Christ, a participation in the love of Father, Son and Spirit. Grace is an aspect of this participation. It is an essential aspect, since we use the word grace to describe the gift of God whereby we are enabled to participate in his life. And as we saw in Chapter 1, grace is also used to mean the act of God whereby we – as Christians – are given the ability to be more than we could manage left to ourselves. Grace, we have seen, is cruciform: it contradicts us but also embraces us.

Thomas Aquinas

Christians talk of grace in different ways. These varied sorts of speaking are sometimes called 'divisions' or 'types' of grace. We will see such divisions at work by examining the ideas of one of the most influential thinkers to dwell on the subject, the thirteenth-century Dominican St Thomas Aquinas (1225–74).

Aquinas wants to help us order our talk of God's action, and this will help us learn more about ourselves as Christians. It is a good thing if people perform good actions, but fallen humanity needs much more. It needs the healing power of grace, which is the act of the Holy Spirit in uniting the believer to Christ. This must come first. Consequent upon this act – upon the believer being 'justified' – are all sorts of other possibilities. There are many things a Christian can do that constitute living out the life of grace, but that life must have been initiated by an act of divine love, according to Aquinas.

For Aquinas, we identify the actions of God in worldly terms, according to the effects that we perceive in this world – this is the only frame of reference we have. So we use language of before and after, even though God is outside time. God's grace is initiating, it sets something up, it comes before our action. This precedence explains one particular term: prevenient grace, grace that 'comes before'. Aquinas relates this priority to the story of salvation in the New Testament. The passion of Christ is the focus of God's saving act for all people, and a consequence of Christ's death, resurrection and ascension is, as the Fourth Gospel says, the coming of the Spirit who breathes into the Church the new life that God in Christ has created.

Our inability to talk adequately of God is related to our need for grace. Human beings can truly know things without grace (though they cannot truly know things without God: the creator is the source of all 'intellectual light'), but they cannot, without the particular assistance of grace, go beyond their finite selves to share in the love that God has in store for them. They need to be raised above themselves. This is a practical consideration and reflection upon the human condition, a reflection to which different responses might be made.

One response – with which Aquinas was familiar – is what came to be called 'semi-Pelagianism'. Theological jargon, at times, can be truly bizarre. The word 'Pelagian' came to mean the idea that a person can earn his or her justification by meritorious acts. (As we now know, this is not what Pelagius himself argued, but the Christian tradition used the term nevertheless.) A 'semi-Pelagian' view is a slight watering down of that notion, with the suggestion that while people manifestly cannot do anything good enough to earn their own salvation, they are able to do their best, and that is enough. If that effort is made, God may look kindly upon it and transform it into the infinite goodness that he himself requires. This interpretation of the relationship between grace and human effort is sometimes referred to with a Latin tag – *quod in se est*: a person is required to do 'that which is within himself'. According to this view, doing that much is a preparation for God's transforming act of grace.

Aquinas, however, rejects the idea. (He explicitly refers to the term *quod in se est* – Aquinas, *Summa Theologiae* 1a 2ae 109, 6.) Since God is not something within the created order that any human effort can reach, it cannot be the case that the human will is able, of itself, to make any preparation for the divine. To do so would be to anticipate God. But I cannot anticipate God since according to Aquinas I can have no understanding of the creative love of God except that which God gives in grace. Were it otherwise, we would descend into an infinite regress whereby I was always being prepared for God so that I could be prepared for God, and so on and so on.

This detail of theological history is more important than we might think, because of Aquinas's choice of language to describe God's act. He employs an understanding of actions and causes (often associated with Aristotle) based upon the idea of movement. This 'efficient causation' is akin to an object pushing another and setting it in motion.

The initiative, the 'push' in the act of grace, can never be anything other than God himself, according to Aquinas. Why is this important? Because it rules out the teaching that we can take the initiative and earn our justification, a teaching that many during the Protestant Reformation attributed to the Catholic Church.

Organizing the language of grace

Aquinas helps us to consider the context for talk about grace, and assists us in organizing our ideas about God so that we do not mislead ourselves into thinking that the act of grace is anything other than a divine act. But he also helps us to organize our talk of grace itself. One might use the word grace to talk of love of someone – being in someone's good graces, we would say today. One might, and Christians usually do, use the word to refer to a free gift – recall the term 'grace and favour', which still refers in some monarchies to properties owned by the monarch and given freely to others for use. Or one might use the word grace to refer to the gratitude such a gift instils – this is the sense of saying 'grace' at meals. The continuation or application of these terms today is not as important as their complementary differences. The first use reminds us more of attitude, our feelings towards someone regardless of any response on their part. But talk of gift is rather different. A significant aspect of gift is the difference it brings about in the recipient. Grace is the gift of God, and it is something active, and something that makes a difference.

Aquinas thinks it sensible to use the language of grace to talk about different ways in which the love of God is at work within our lives. He distinguishes, for example, between 'sanctifying grace' and 'gratuitous grace' (or 'grace freely bestowed' – no English rendering of this Latin term fails to be awkward). The former – sanctifying grace – is, as its name suggests, that which brings about the justification of an individual, causing them to return to fellowship with the divine. 'Grace freely bestowed' does the same, but it is different from 'sanctifying grace' because its object is not the person who receives it, but another person (*Summa Theologiae* 1a 2ae 111, 1). It is the grace one receives in order to assist the sanctification of someone else. It is correctly called grace because only God can work to bring about fellowship with himself. But it is differentiated from 'sanctifying grace' because, by using a different term, we can remind ourselves that God works in and through the world he has created. That creation includes people and relationships, which can – through this grace – co-operate with the divine will to bring about the union of love into which Christians are baptized.

'Co-operate' is another important word, and marks one half of the distinction between 'operative' and 'co-operative' grace. A plain reading of these words might leave us thinking that 'operative' grace is what God does and 'co-operative grace' is what we do. However, only God can be the cause of grace. So instead, Aquinas encourages us to think of two different ways of speaking about human action. We might call them 'willing' and 'doing'. God, as the creative source of motion, moves the will by his creative act of love: this is 'operative' grace. The human being, moved by grace to will the goodness of God, might then act in accordance with that will. In other words, he or she might do what God commands. If so, that act is both truly the action of that person and also truly the action of God ('co-operative grace').

Aquinas thinks that we should also understand grace to be 'habitual'. By this he means that grace imparts a condition whereby we are disposed to act in particular ways. This 'habit' or 'disposition' is characteristic of the Christian, and it is solely the result of grace. It is the result of 'operative grace', because God gives us the disposition to will and act as Christians should. It is also the result of 'co-operative grace' because – having that disposition – we are enabled to act well, to be charitable, generous, and so on.

Earlier mention was made of 'prevenient grace', grace that 'comes before'. Aquinas thinks that we should also speak in terms of 'subsequent grace', grace which follows after. Why? In answer to that question he offers a succinct list of 'five effects of grace in us': 'Firstly, the healing of the soul; secondly, willing the good; thirdly, the efficacious performance of the good willed; fourthly, perseverance in the good; fifthly, the attainment of glory.' He goes on:

> And so, in that it causes the first effect in us, grace is called prevenient with respect to the second effect; and in that it causes the second effect in us, it is called subsequent with respect to the first. And as a single effect is posterior to one effect and prior to another, so grace can be called both prevenient and subsequent in regard to the same effect, under different respects. (*Summa Theologiae* 1a 2ae 111, 3).

Readers unfamiliar with this style of theology might find it strange. (It's sometimes called 'scholastic', though that term only really means according to a school, and there were lots of 'schools' of theology in the Middle Ages, just as there are now.) How does this careful description and analysis of grace as Aquinas understands it help us learn more about the loving act of God? The answer, I think, is contained in the short passage quoted. The subject of Aquinas's concern is something thoroughly practical. Look again at his list of the effects of grace. We might paraphrase it: the healing of our spiritual sickness; our wanting the good; our managing to do it; our managing to continue doing it; and finally our coming home to the vision of God in his eternal presence. Note that all of these are 'our' actions. But because they are all the effects of grace, they are also God's actions.

Another medieval theologian

Aquinas is among the most celebrated Christian writers on grace, but the divisions and seeming precision that we find in his writing is far from unique to him. The relationship between God's loving mercy and the human failure to love is so basic and fundamental an aspect of Christian theology that few theologians have ignored it, and by the time that Aquinas came to write, a substantial tradition of debate and definition concerning grace already existed. However, we should recall the earlier warning against assuming that the thinkers of the past saw these as principally intellectual issues. They are concerned to articulate the realities of the Christian life.

We might make a contrast of style with another famous medieval writer, Julian of Norwich, who in her 'Shewings' or revelations of Divine Love, compares the human condition – represented by the sin of Adam – with the relationship between a master and a servant:

> The lord looks upon his servant very lovingly and sweetly and mildly. He sends him to a certain place to do his will. Not only does the servant go, but he dashes off and runs

at great speed, loving to do his lord's will. And soon he falls into a dell and is greatly injured: and then he groans and moans and tosses about and writhes, but he cannot rise or help himself in any way. And of all this, the greatest hurt which I saw him in was lack of consolation, for he could not turn his face to look on his loving lord, who was very close to him, in whom is all consolation; but like a man who was for the time extremely feeble and foolish, he paid heed to his feelings and his continuing distress . . . (Julian of Norwich, *Showings,* p. 267)

The servant, desperate to do his master's will, runs off so excitedly that he slips and falls and – so desolate is he at his failure to do what was asked – groans, moans, wails and writhes in his fallen condition, but is unable to pick himself up. But his greatest lack is his inability, in all his self-loathing, to turn to his master, for were he to do so he would see his Lord next to him, stooping to help him up.

This is a popular tale, from a work of theological literature altogether different in style from the writings of Aquinas. But its content is closer than we think. The story of the master and the servant is a parable of salvation – Julian identifies the servant with Adam, the type of humanity – but it also speaks to us of the common human experience of trying and failing, of wanting to do well but being unable to do so. This is a helpful illustration of the Christian life. Aquinas is writing in a different context to that of Julian's visionary meditations, but he too is expressing, through his questions and classifications, the reality of life in Christ. Both theologies are rooted in the self-giving love of God, both are undergirded by the notion of God the creator, and both spell out the essence of grace – that God gives himself freely to bring created humanity into closer union with the divine. And both do so by illustrating the essential practicality of the Christian life.

Grace as Christian experience

These practicalities are the basis for dividing the language of grace. The technical terms 'prevenient' and 'subsequent' are a good example. There simply are some things in the Christian life that follow on from other things. Exercise and fitness might be compared. A person might have to begin a programme of physical exercise in order to become physically fit. That would be step one. Having become much fitter, they would then need to continue with some sort of habitual exercise (almost certainly different) in order to stay that way. That would be a subsequent step. This is what life is like. St Paul knew the same thing, and it is no surprise to find Aquinas giving examples of the distinctions he makes by referring to the variety of gifts given by the one Spirit, which Paul outlines in his writings to the Corinthians.

Another division we encountered in Aquinas was that between the grace that transforms an individual, and the individual's part in the wider network of Christian relationships that might help to bring about the transformation of another. This is similarly practical. In both cases, God is at work as creator, as the one bringing something from nothing, infusing or setting alight 'operative' grace – enabling a human being to be united with the life of God. And God the creator works not just in the single moments we perceive, but continuously to bring about good, so that the actions that are enabled by grace are then brought to fruition by the 'co-operative' grace that remains God's action and is also and truly your action and mine. All these divisions of grace, we might then say, are different ways of talking about 'Christian experience'.

These thoughts might help us to avoid reducing grace to its consequences. Grace is more than a word we use to fill in a gap between human failure and divine love. Christian theology maintains that that gap is indeed filled. But it is not filled by a concept, it is filled by an act – the loving act of God which brings something from nothing. Just as God's action in creation brings about those things we call real (and hence why sin and evil are, in this sense, unreal) the consequences of grace are real. And it is easier to talk about those consequences – about what it means to act well, or how it might be that I can make true statements about the unknowable God – than it is to articulate the creative act of God's love. Difficulty of expression does not diminish the reality of that love, however, and hence it does not diminish the real acts of grace that we identify in particular ways and particular experiences as human beings.

In the most celebrated of Aquinas's many writings, the *Summa Theologiae*, the discussion of grace immediately precedes a discussion of the theological virtues, faith, hope and charity. The ordering is deliberate. Grace works itself out in human lives, by effecting real changes in real people. The consequences of these changes are the dispositions to act in accordance with the will of God, which we call virtues. Faith, the first of these, is an act that is mine, but also God's, in that my ability to attain the intellectual knowledge of that which is infinitely beyond my capacities is only possible by grace. This 'knowledge' is not, however, the kind of knowing that applies to most of our experiences – I might 'know' that $7 \times 5 = 35$, or that Tony Blair won the 1997 general election, through some fairly normal means of human learning. Faith, according to Aquinas and others, consists in my being united with the object of my faith. The grace that enables me to participate in the life of God becomes the vehicle for my 'knowing' not a fact, but the source of all truth. Knowing God then enables me to 'know' everything else in the light of this fundamental illumination.

The greatest consequence of grace in the life of any person is, according to Aquinas, love of God, or charity. There are different words for 'love' in the Christian tradition. Charity translates the Latin *caritas*, which itself features in the Latin Vulgate (the Bible used by Aquinas and other western theologians of the Middle Ages), as the equivalent of the Greek word *agapē* – the love that Paul describes in I Corinthians 13. This is the self-giving love that is manifest in the teaching of Jesus, and personified in his life, death and resurrection. All theological virtue, all the power a person has to act in accordance with the will of God, is directed by charity because charity is a communion with God, a participation in the divine nature. Charity is the form of all virtues because in loving God we love the good. Our wills are directed towards the God who is love, the definition of right action.

A history of hydraulics

These different ways of thinking about grace have differing implications for the way we think about the impact of God's life upon our own. Thomas Aquinas was writing well before the sixteenth-century Reformation, but not in a united Church. The division between Christian East and West has often led people to suggest a radical difference in the understanding of grace between Western Catholicism and Eastern Orthodoxy. So, for example, some speak of the distinction between 'created' and 'uncreated' grace. Of course, nothing is 'uncreated' except God himself and so, in the teaching of Gregory Palamas (1296–1359), uncreated grace should be identified with the divine energies. These are the knowable divine works (distinct from the unknowable divine essence), which are nevertheless truly God himself. Western theology was not unfamiliar with this distinction (Aquinas makes rich use of the eighth-century Byzantine theologian John of Damascus, who writes of the divine energies), and few theologians would have denied that it makes sense to speak of uncreated grace, because one necessary way of thinking about grace is as God himself giving himself: another way of thinking and of talking about the act of God that – as properly creative – is properly indescribable.

Protestant theology too has made much of different sorts of grace and, as we saw in the last chapter, the influence of Augustine on John Calvin and those who followed him is highly significant. Some Reformed theologians write about 'common grace', which is opposed to 'special grace'. The first of these is something that is available to all people, a gift of God's love in creation, the recipients of which are all whom God creates. 'Special grace' is, like the 'sanctifying grace' of Aquinas, the particular gift of God that moves the will and brings about the justification of the sinner. Early Protestantism found itself divided over the consequences of God's grace, and its relationship to the human will. We already know that a notion of grace opposed to free will is bound to be controversial. There is a risk in the assumption that divine and human willing can be thought of as belonging to the same order or framework. If they do, the love of God might be seen not as gracious but tyrannical. This danger led followers of the Dutch theologian Jacobus Arminius (including many seventeenth-century English theologians) to maintain that, although salvation cannot be earned, it must also be possible for a human person, by his or her will, finally to resist the grace of God. In a famous sermon preached in Bristol Cathedral, John Wesley emphasized that the grace of God is sovereign in justifying the sinner but also that the necessity of God's sustaining love is clear. All human beings – including those justified by grace – can make the wrong choices and hence can fall away.

These apparently endless possibilities for classifying and understanding grace are too often concerned with what some call the 'hydraulics of grace', a technical fascination with conceptual distinction and debate that seems removed from the Christian life. Though his writing might seem unfamiliar, Thomas Aquinas is not guilty of this removal, and neither are the great theologians of the East, nor the Protestant preachers of the sixteenth and seventeenth centuries, nor the prophets of the Evangelical Revival. Grace must be seen as something practical, as something that gives expression to what it means to be a Christian.

Grace and discipleship

This practicality is the subject of one of the classic theological works of the twentieth century, Dietrich Bonhoeffer's *Discipleship* (the German is simply *Nachfolgen*, 'discipleship', though it is often known in English by the title of its first translation – *The Cost of Discipleship*). Bonhoeffer at first seems to come down surprisingly hard on the theological concept of grace. His work begins with the words, 'Cheap grace is the mortal enemy of our church. Our struggle today is for costly grace.' Cheap grace is, for Bonhoeffer, grace without consequences, a general proclamation of forgiveness, the guarantee of the price 'paid in advance for all time'. Grace becomes the comfort for the sinner who does not have to try, who conforms the Church to the world and offers a free for all of love in which none of the choices we make makes any difference. It is the affirmation of the living for ourselves that is characteristic of a selfish world. 'Cheap grace is that grace which we bestow on ourselves.'

> Cheap grace is preaching forgiveness without repentance; it is baptism without the discipline of community; it is the Lord's supper without the confession of sin; it is absolution without personal confession. Cheap grace is grace without discipleship, grace without the cross, grace without the living incarnate Jesus Christ. (Bonhoeffer, *Discipleship*, p. 44).

Bonhoeffer's fear is that the declaration of grace as a doctrine – the love of God as an idea rather than an actuality – lets Christians off the hook. The Church was too ready to conform to the world, but bolstered this conformity by setting up a separate sphere of holiness – monasticism – which shut the activity of discipleship off from the world in which human beings are called. The Reformation he sees as in part a response to this compartmentalization, but it brought its own hazards. If we follow the Reformers, and stress the absolute graciousness of God in justifying me, a sinner, we are in danger of creating for ourselves an easy Christianity, whereby my life can be lived as I choose because of the safety net of salvation that my faith in Christ provides. To avoid this danger, Bonhoeffer suggests, we should think of grace as something costly, something that demands obedience, something that has very real and very practical consequences.

Bonhoeffer does not regard grace as something for which one strives, as if one can gain grace by doing particular things. Grace is the gift of God in Christ. It is costly because it entails striving, but one is only able to strive as a Christian because that grace comes first. More importantly, however, that grace is costly not first of all to me, but first of all to the God who chooses to enter into my world, to embrace all that my sin and weakness costs, and to bear that cost in suffering and death in order to overcome it.

> It is costly, because it calls to discipleship; it is grace, because it calls us to follow Jesus Christ. It is costly because it costs people their lives; it is grace because it thereby makes them live. It is costly because it condemns sin; it is grace because it justifies the sinner. Above all, grace is costly because it was costly to God, because it cost God the life of God's son . . . Above all, it is grace because the life of God's Son was not too costly for God to give in order to make us live. God did, indeed, give him up for us. Costly grace is the incarnation of God. (Bonhoeffer, *Discipleship*, p. 45).

Grace, for Bonhoeffer, is the call to discipleship. The first disciples are called to act, to do something. In the case of the fishermen summoned from their nets, they are called so that they themselves may call, may catch other fish in their miraculous net. A practical theology of grace requires that all are called to act, and that people are called to do specific things, to act as Christians in the world and towards those around them, not to think thoughts of abstract virtue or to detach themselves from what they find uncongenial or worldly. Bonhoeffer, in fact, insists on what he calls the this-wordliness of Christianity. In a letter written in prison he tells his friend how previously he had thought that one could acquire faith by living a holy or saintly life but that he had come to realize that such attempts take us apart from the world, and it is within the world that Christ's call is heard, by us as by those ordinary working fishermen. By this worldliness, Bonhoeffer says he means

> living unreservedly in life's duties, problems, successes and failures, experiences and perplexities. In so doing we throw ourselves completely into the arms of God, taking seriously not our own sufferings, but those of God in the world, watching with Christ in Gethsemane. That, I think, is faith. (Bonhoeffer, *Letters and Papers from Prison*, pp. 369–70).

Bonhoeffer allows us to repeat the contention set out at the beginning of this book. Grace is not something abstract. Discipleship is emphasized not simply because people are called to do something real in the real world around them, but because people are called by Jesus Christ, by the God who identifies himself with that world. They are called by the God who is not detached and remote, not to be reached by separation and transcendence, but who is always God for and with us, here and now, not in abstract but in the concrete realities of worldly life – the events, the relationships, the tasks, the failures, the efforts that characterize human life. Christian discussion of grace is a discussion of the ways in which that call to discipleship is lived out in the community we call the Church. The call to follow Christ is a call to act in the world, in this life, because it is in this life that God comes to us in Christ and reveals himself to us as one among us, as he revealed himself to peasant fisherman by the Galilean lakeside. The Church is the name we give to the corporate discipleship of believers, and its teaching and practice (the doctrine that it does, we might say) is reflection about discipleship. The word discipleship means 'learning', and so what the Christian community says and does is the articulation of its process of learning, of learning what it means to participate in the divine life, to live in the power of the Spirit. Living is something practical, and so grace is something practical.

Operating and co-operating

There is a crude distinction we might make between a Catholic view of grace – one concerned with the Church and the sacraments, and the corporate life of the Church – and a Protestant view – one concerned with the justification of the individual. In both cases, the spectre of Pelagius and of the Reformation haunts our discussion, because we are too ready to set God up in opposition to humanity, as if this were a contest between two persons, one good and strong, the other bad and weak. Seeing these issues in terms of simple opposites will lead us to the controversies that divided interpreters of Calvin in the seventeenth century, just as they divided readers of Augustine more than a thousand years earlier.

As we saw when considering the notion of 'merit', however, these divisions need not be so decisive. I have suggested throughout this book that grace is 'cruciform'. It has an oppositional aspect, one that confounds humanity because the perfect self-giving love of God is contrary to the human desire for self. But because grace enables us to participate in the divine life, it also has a relational aspect, it embraces and envelops us in the love of God that is perfect relatedness. It is this both/and sense of grace that we must retain. To say that grace is something we must earn is to deny that God's love is truly creative; to say that the free gift of grace leaves us with no response or responsibility is to set God in opposition to the world that he created in love. God's initiative is always paramount, because, however much we may not wish to, we must let God be God. But God the creator is not the kind of God who starts things off and lets them go like clockwork (or otherwise). Instead God is at work in all that is real, drawing out the response to grace that is called Christian discipleship.

Feeling new strength

As before, music can come to our aid. A great deal of music is structured around some variant of what is known as 'ternary form', a simple presentation of an idea, followed by something different, followed by a reversion to the original idea. There are many different ways in which this basic structure can be played out, one of the best known being sonata form, which is often described using the terms 'exposition', 'development' and 'recapitulation'. The expression of something, followed by the breaking in of something else is – for many people – a useful image of the grace of God. Charles Wesley's wonderful hymn 'And can it be, that I should gain an interest in the Saviour's blood?'

(*Hymns and Psalms*, no. 216), for example, speaks powerfully in scriptural terms of the imprisoned spirit:

> Long my imprisoned spirit lay,
> Fast bound in sin and nature's night;
> Thine eye diffused a quickening ray –
> I woke, the dungeon flamed with light;
> My chains fell off, my heart was free,
> I rose, went forth, and followed Thee.
> My chains fell off, my heart was free,
> I rose, went forth, and followed Thee.

This style of Christian poetry is often related only to the experience of conversion, or 'becoming a Christian', and it draws upon the powerful and dramatic theology of grace and the justification of the sinner that we find in writers such as Martin Luther. But divine grace, amazing as it is according to Wesley's contemporary John Newton, is not restricted to this moment. It crosses the believer over and over again as he or she attempts to be a disciple, to learn from Jesus of Nazareth by living the Christian life.

In the year 1825 Ludwig van Beethoven, already well over 50, found himself seriously ill and feared that he would die. Upon recovering he wrote a wordless hymn of thanksgiving which became the third movement of his String Quartet no. 15, opus 132, in A minor. That movement is entitled 'Hymn of thanksgiving from a convalescent to the Godhead', and consists of three slow chorale-like sections, interspersed with two faster passages over which Beethoven wrote the words 'feeling new strength'. The heavenly solemnity of the chorale ideas, and their interruption by the sparkling dance-like sections, combine to provide some of the most extraordinarily powerful and beautiful music ever produced.

The image is probably clear – stately human steps are burst in upon by the grace of God that gives new strength. But to restrict the analogue of grace to that interaction would be to miss much of the richness Beethoven offers. Each time the new, faster passage is heard, it is followed by a return to the original idea which is both the same (it is the original idea) and different – different because it must sound differently having been preceded by the interruption, and different because Beethoven works into his initial chorale a greater complexity each time it returns. This increased complexity is imitative of the 'feeling new strength' theme by its introduction of faster harmonic progressions as the three other instruments support the first violin walking, tone by tone, within the Lydian mode (the scale beginning on F, but including B natural, in which Beethoven wrote this movement). The second idea has, in other words, affected the first. And not just because it has broken in upon it and interrupted it, but because it has worked itself inside that first idea, and caused it to become the more complex and the more ravishing as a result.

It has confounded, and also embraced, as does grace. But it has also been enacted, or rather played out, in the ongoing development of the movement. It weaves its magic in relationship with the rest of the music into which it flows. It is not a single moment, or a lone musical idea, it is a creative gift that continues to bear fruit as the music continues to play. In 1931, writing to his friend Stephen Spender, the poet T. S. Eliot recorded listening to this piece and said of Beethoven, 'There is a sort of heavenly, or at least more than human gaiety, about some of his later things.' Human, and also more than human: such is the life of grace we call discipleship.

8

Grace and the image of God in human beings

A new creation

The letter to the Galatians was written in controversial circumstances. Paul fired it off in dispute with those who insisted that Gentile Christians must be made subject to the full physical requirements of the ritual law. Their demand was that Gentiles must be circumcised before they could be brought into the Kingdom of those redeemed by Christ. For Paul, as we saw in Chapter 2, this insistence denies the freedom to which believers are called, because it creates a physical barrier between Christ and the nations. The law remains the gift of God – our guardian through infancy and education, as he puts it (Galatians 3.24) – but now that the law has come to its completion, its fruition in Christ, the physical demands that mark out God's chosen people have also come to an end. To have subjected the Gentile Christians to circumcision would have been to subject them to the whole law, but to do that would be to suggest that Christ had lived and died to no purpose.

Rather than physical requirements, Paul urges his hearers to attend to the desires of the Spirit. Life in the Spirit is the true freedom of every Christian, the freedom to live out the love of God poured into our hearts through Christ. Those who look to the physical can boast, or, as he puts it, can glory in their physical identity and accomplishments. Paul's response to such glorying is unequivocal: 'Far be it from me to glory except in the cross of our Lord Jesus Christ, by which the world has been crucified to me, and I to the world' (Galatians 6.14 RSV). Paul is contradicting his opponents, who are boasting in the physical, the things of this material life. But he is making that contradiction by boasting in something else which is physical and something else which is human: the cross of Jesus Christ. That physical thing, and that human person, however, are the stuff not of life but of death. The cross is the instrument of execution, its owner is the victim who suffered for the sins of the world. So the worldly boasts of human life are excluded by something that brings not life but death, something that brings humanity not to glory but to destruction. If I glory, I do so in the cross by which the world has been crucified to me and I to the world: the things of worldly life have come to an end because of the cross of Christ. My own life is no more, the physical life of the world around me has been brought to nothing. If Paul glories in the world and in humanity, he does so because of something that displays, as clearly as can be, the ability of the world to be genuinely evil. The cross reminds us that the world can turn its back on the love of God, to abuse and nullify the life and the world that God has created.

Paul's theology seems bizarre, and it is meant to be. Another verse tells us why: there is neither circumcision, nor uncircumcision, but a new creation (Galatians 6.15). The world that was ruled by the physical has come to an end. There is 'a new creation': the life and the death of Christ have brought about not just a change in the old order, not just the fulfilment of the hopes of the people of Israel, but something so topsy-turvey, so disordered that it can only be described by the term 'a new creation'. What is being implied is not so much that everything has been transformed, but that everything has been made all over again. All things have been created anew, brought from the nothing of death into the everything that is the life of God in the Spirit. All this has come about through the life and death of Christ. Jesus of Nazareth, the one whose life incarnates, lives out as human, the very Spirit of love that is the life of God himself. The absurdity of Paul's gospel of grace is that the death of the one who himself was nothing but life has brought eternal life and freedom to the world that was enslaved by the physical care of self and material gain. The death of Christ has brought about a new creation; it has brought new life, a new something, from the nothing of absence and failure that marked human inability to live up to the demands of the law.

The something it has brought, the new creation of which Paul speaks, is life in the Spirit, human participation in the life of God. At the very beginning of the book of Genesis the earth was without form and void, and the Spirit of God moved on the face of the waters. God's creative presence is the presence of love that we call the Holy Spirit, and that Spirit is the agent of creation, the one whose power in the beginning brought light from darkness, and the earth from formless void. Now, in Jesus Christ, this creative Spirit brings a new life of love to all who receive the grace of God, because genuine love is always creative, and always bringing about new possibilities.

This contrast of old and new reminds us of the dramatic and oppositional understanding of grace that we found in Martin Luther. His theology of grace was greatly influenced by his reading of Galatians. The language of conversion in classical Protestant theology makes much of contrast. Our continued insistence that grace is cruciform plays upon a similar idea: grace crosses humanity, because the perfect love of God contradicts the disordered desires of the human self. However, when we speak of 'new creation', we might reasonably ask ourselves what was wrong with the old one. If, as we have repeatedly stated, it is only the love of God that is truly creative, why need God create anew? Is there something about humanity on its own, something about the nature of what it is to be a human person, that is deficient? Should the created order be thought of as existing without grace? Might this help us better appreciate the generosity of God's act in bestowing grace, in freely giving the gift of his life to those who are baptized? And if so, what sense should Christian teaching make of the notion that God created humanity 'in his own image' (Genesis 1.28)?

Grace and nature

We touch here upon some of the most substantial debates in twentieth-century theology. Karl Barth, whom we encountered in Chapter 6, found himself reacting to a long-standing tendency in theological writing to assume that the truth about God was best found by looking first at the world and the human situation within it. Fearing that Christian writers were in danger of creating God in their own image, Barth went out of his way to emphasize the infinite distance between God and creation. We cannot contain the maker of all things in the things that are made. However, that correcting emphasis created problems as well as solving them, because if God cannot be adequately conceived of or known by men and women, how is it possible for people to speak about him at all? The answer, Barth suggested, lay with God himself. God's act must always come first. God can be known if he chooses to make himself known. He does this in his act of revelation, by speaking his Word, Jesus Christ, who is witnessed to by scripture and proclaimed by the Church.

Barth's understanding of revelation is perhaps the most influential modern theological idea. This does not mean, however, that all agreed. Barth reacted fiercely to the suggestion of one colleague, Emil Brunner, that there remained a point of contact between God and human beings. This link, Brunner felt, enabled humanity to receive the revelation that God offered. Barth addressed this idea in a polemical essay to which he gave the title 'No!' Brunner's claim, he argued, must distort our knowledge of God. It had to mean that there was a second source of revelation, some other grounds for knowledge of God other than God's manifestation of himself in Jesus Christ. If we could know God by any other means, then the adequacy of God's own revelation would be called into question.

Part of the issue here is the interpretation of a passage in the first chapter of Genesis, in which we read:

Then God said, 'Let us make humankind in our image, according to our likeness; and let them have dominion over the fish of the sea, and over the birds of the air, and over the cattle, and over all the wild animals of the earth, and over every creeping thing that creeps upon the earth.' So God created humankind in his image, in the image of God he created them; male and female he created them. (Genesis 1.26–27)

It is this biblical doctrine of the image of God in which human beings were created that Brunner felt he was upholding by insisting on a point of contact between God and humanity. Brunner agreed with Barth that the fallen state of humanity is complete; there is nothing in men and women that is not affected by sin. However, he also pointed to those things that distinguished humanity from other animals – rationality and responsibility – and suggested that these meant that the image of God was not obliterated by sin. Human need of the grace of God is absolute, but men and women retain the capacity to receive that grace. This, Brunner felt, is what is meant by the difference between human beings and other creatures.

The essay of Brunner's to which Barth angrily reacted (he himself chose the word 'angry' to describe the beginning of his response) is pointedly entitled 'Nature and Grace.' These words suggest not the Protestant Reformed tradition of those two Swiss theologians, but the Catholic or 'Thomist' theology that rooted itself in the writings of Aquinas. In opposition to the view that human nature is entirely corrupt, one often hears quoted some words of St Thomas: 'Grace does not destroy nature, but perfects it' (*Summa Theologiae* 1a 1, 8). Some take this as implying that grace and humanity should be thought of as entirely separate, before the initiative of God brings them together. The idea here is that human beings exist naturally, without grace, and then are the recipients of an addition, the gift of grace that builds upon nature to make a 'two-storey' composite.

The French Jesuit thinker Henri de Lubac objected to this reading of Aquinas. He felt that the Catholic Church's teaching on grace had allowed itself to be distorted from its original assumptions by the debates of the Reformation.

The need to oppose a view of the utter corruption of humanity had led some to defend the idea of a pure human nature that was not entirely without goodness. This 'pure nature' was then bound to be seen as entirely distinct from grace. Grace became thought of as something that had nothing to do with human beings as created by God, but only came as an add-on, a gift given by God to humanity rather as one very wealthy and powerful person might give something to another person whose need was great. Understanding grace in this way meant that grace was conceived as an object being handed over, as it were, rather than the creative action of God.

The Christian tradition, according to de Lubac, assumed a rather different understanding of human nature. Human beings, being created in the image of God, were – by virtue of that creation – destined for the union with God that grace brings about. Human beings are directed towards union with their creator because – simply by being created – human beings participate in the gift of God, their very existence. The destiny of human beings is, according to Thomas Aquinas among many others, to enjoy the beatific vision, to be raised to the presence of God by the grace that unites them with Christ. If it is part of the nature of human beings to be united with God by grace, a simple division between nature and grace is fundamentally misleading.

We can see now, I hope, why this chapter began with a reflection upon Paul's language of a new creation. If God is the creator – if everything that exists depends for every moment of its existence upon the creative love of God – then that which is created cannot be utterly opposed to grace. Simply by being alive, by existing (or, as many theologians insist, by 'being'), human beings are sharing in the gift of God's love. One way in which that gift has been interpreted by Christians is through the Old Testament notion of the 'image of God'. The natural world is not entire and complete of itself. The natural world is God's creation, and its goal is the life of grace.

Grace and infinity

Another modern interpreter of Thomas Aquinas who wanted to rethink the traditional separation of grace and nature was the German Karl Rahner. He offered an account of being human that depended upon his understanding of grace. Rahner sets this out, in rather complex terms, by describing the human activity of knowing. In knowing any particular thing as particular, human beings presuppose the infinite. What does this mean? It is not as complicated as it sounds. If I look at a chair and recognize it to be a chair, I have not recognized it to be a dog. Neither have I recognized it to be a footballer, a symphony, a coral reef or a kettle. In fact, if we follow this logic through, by identifying a chair as a chair, I have unconsciously rejected the possibility that it is anything else, I have picked the concept 'chair' from an infinite number of possible concepts I could have chosen to apply to that object. Now of course when I know that something is a chair, my mind is not going through the processes I have just set out. It is simply identifying a chair. But there remain the possibilities that a particular thing might be all sorts of other particular things, and those possibilities are endless, or infinite. Rahner thinks that God's creative act is the infinite possibility that is being presupposed. So we can only know anything at all because we have what he calls a 'pre-apprehension' of the infinite possibilities of existence.

The human being's place in creation means that he or she is oriented, or directed, towards the infinite mystery we call God. This does not mean, for Rahner, that a person knows God 'in advance', as it were. It means that there is something about humanity that makes us talk about the grace of God. Human beings are able to receive grace, and they are able to receive grace because God has created them to do so.

Rahner insists that theology is subject to the utterly mysterious nature of the divine. By mystery he does not mean something that can in principle be understood or solved, as we tend to use the term. For us, a mystery is a puzzle that requires a detective to figure out. For the theologian, however, the mystery of God is the impossibility of confining God the creator within the terms of that creation. To do so is to reduce the reality of God to an anthropomorphized idol of our own making. Such an error is not merely intellectually indefensible, it is biblically inexcusable. We would be no better than the makers of objects for idol worship, who are so mercilessly lampooned by the writer whom we call Second Isaiah. Mystery must be the basis of all talk about God, because only a theology that knows its own limits can hope to avoid being misleading.

Like de Lubac, Rahner uses the word 'supernatural' to rework the old distinction between nature and grace. To think of human nature entirely apart from grace is to think of something that can never be true. Nature is only a 'remainder concept': we can conceive of it only as a thought experiment. We can talk about the activity of grace in directing human beings towards the creator, and imagine those human beings without that grace. It is possible, in this thought experiment, to conceive of a human being without thinking about creation: this is what pure nature might be said to be. But human beings are created by God, and hence grace and nature must be brought together. There is something essentially 'supernatural' about created humanity. Human beings exist as they do by the creative love of God.

Anonymous and explicit faith

Grace, then, is part of what makes human beings what they are. The gift of God's infinite love directs human beings towards the mystery of creation, which they unconsciously acknowledge simply by being human. Perhaps Rahner's most famous theological idea follows from this understanding of graced humanity. He makes a distinction between two different types of faith. One he calls 'explicit', and it means something very much like what we all mean when we use the word faith – the relationship of love and trust in God into which one is drawn by being united with Christ. Rahner's other type of faith he calls 'anonymous': this is the novel idea that has caused much discussion. Rahner suggests that, because all human beings are directed towards the infinite in creation, so we can reasonably say that human beings can receive grace without explicitly being part of the traditional Christian community.

Anonymous faith exists when a person accepts God. This can happen when anyone accepts his or her own part in the unlimited potential that God has created. Human beings can open themselves to the infinite. They can accept that the world is more than a world of here and now and me and mine. In this way they can transcend themselves, can move beyond the particular and the limited. They are acknowledging the grace of God in Christ, regardless of whether their awareness of this grace is in any way explicit.

Grace is, for Rahner, 'an abiding possibility of human freedom' (Rahner, *Theological Investigations*, vol. 16, p. 56). Here he inaugurated, perhaps unintentionally, a revolution in Christian theology by suggesting that the graced nature of creation allows us to describe other religious traditions as 'lawful' in so far as they have 'supernatural elements arising out of the grace which is given to men as a gratuitous gift on account of Christ.' (Rahner, *Theological Investigations* vol. 5, p. 121).

Rahner offers us hope when considering a question that had, for most of Christian history, seemed reasonably hopeless. What can we say of the grace of God apart from those who belong to the Body of Christ? Without embarking upon a lengthy explanation to tackle the problem, we can make a few observations. First, we should not see the nature of humanity as something that can be considered apart from its place in God's creation. If Christian faith is reflected in – say – only one-third of the human population, it does not follow from these proportions that there is something wrong with humanity or wrong with creation. The gift of God's love is not deficient. Second, we should be wary of thinking that we can step outside the language and teaching of the Christian tradition and still practise Christian theology. To think of all religious traditions as empirical phenomena which are equally verifiable from some neutral point of view is to do another thought experiment and nothing more. We come to these questions presupposing Christian doctrine: any Christian theology that proceeds on the basis that Christian talk may or may not be worthwhile is not Christian theology. But, third, and perhaps reflecting Rahner, the emphasis of all Christian writers on the gratuitousness of God's love should warn us against thinking that grace can be something closed, or that access to the love of God can be limited. Christian discipleship, as we saw in the last chapter, is the call to learn what it means to live as one who is in Christ. This learning means being led by the Spirit, following God's action: the drawing of this love and the voice of this calling, as the author of the *Cloud of Unknowing* puts it. To live in the Spirit is to be led in faith, not to know in advance the truths of God's mystery. For Rahner, openness to the infinite is openness to grace. For all Christians, openness to the Spirit is a confession that we are always, in some sense, agnostic as to the possibilities of God's love – we simply do not know what God will do.

The crucified God

We return to the idea that human beings are created in the image of God. What does this mean? One possible answer might be found in the contention of this book that grace is cruciform. We began this chapter by reflecting on Paul's letter to the Galatians, in which he uses the phrase 'new creation'. He does so elsewhere as well, when writing to the Corinthian church. The first letter to the Corinthians begins, as we saw in Chapter 3, with Paul's rejection of any worldly or human manner of thinking. All that we know must be transformed by the impossible reality of Christ crucified. This is the beginning of Christian knowledge, the foundation on which Christian teaching is built. In his second epistle to Corinth, Paul asserts his belief that being 'in Christ' means being created anew:

So if anyone is in Christ, there is a new creation: everything old has passed away; see, everything has become new! All this is from God, who reconciled us to himself through Christ, and has given us the ministry of reconciliation; that is, in Christ God was reconciling the world to himself, not counting their trespasses against them, and entrusting the message of reconciliation to us . . . For our sake he made him to be sin who knew no sin, so that in him we might become the righteousness of God. (2 Corinthians 5.17–19, 21)

Uniting our lives to his in Christ, God has brought about the reconciliation of the world to himself. Making the sinless Son into the type of sinful humanity, and thereby restoring the broken relationship between creator and created, God has turned on its head the opposition between human self and the self-giving love of the Trinity poured out for human beings on the cross of Christ. The human self is now drawn in to participate in that self-giving love, and that participation is the life of grace.

However, once again we come up against the problems of being human: the contrast between that which we might do, and that which we manage. Human beings have the capacity for self-giving, but rarely the inclination. The incarnation 'crosses' humanity with divine love by enacting a perfectly human perfect self-giving in the life, death and resurrection of Christ. The archetype of the image of God, for Christians, must therefore be the person of Jesus Christ and the image of self-giving that he projects. To be human is to be created, already existing only within the confines of the grace of God. To know oneself as created in the image of God is to know oneself as an imitator of Christ. It means crossing the law of self with the law of love so that the best of our potential is realized in our worldly human lives, and not simply in the hope of a heavenly future.

The cruciform image of God

The life of grace we have called discipleship, and it is
hardly a surprise that in the Gospels those who would follow Jesus are called to take up their cross. The meeting of
heaven and earth that we find in the person of Christ is the
unity of creation and reconciliation that we have insisted
underlie our Christian doctrine of grace. Two famous paintings can help us here, not least because the second borrows
from the first. Call to mind – or look at, perhaps online –
the well-known image of the 'Creation of Adam' from
Michelangelo's series of frescoes on the ceiling of the Sistine
Chapel in Rome. Two arms are outstretched towards the
centre of the picture. One of them – the creative arm of
God – is strong and dynamic in appearance. The arm of
the human Adam is limp by contrast, awaiting the divine
creative spark. That life-giving touch is about to take place,
and it is portrayed as a metaphor for the love of God in creation, since God – visually represented – is forced to stretch
out from himself in order to give what is his alone to give –
life itself – to the lifeless person.

Around a century later, another Michelangelo – Michelangelo
Merisi, better known as Caravaggio – reminded onlookers
of the creation of Adam when painting his canvas the *Call
of St Matthew*, which hangs, with two other paintings of
the evangelist, in the Church of San Luigi dei Francesi – the
French church – in Rome. The contrasts in this picture –
again well worth examining on something like the Web
Gallery of Art – bring out the essentially cruciform nature of
the life to which Matthew, the tax collector, is being called.

This painting presents two contrasting groupings. On the
left, the tax booth, or money table, where Matthew and his
companions are counting their ill-gotten gains, ill-gotten because

they are profiting personally from collecting the taxes imposed by the occupying power. Bags of money – perhaps pieces of silver – are seen on the table. The two figures on the extreme left look down, one peering almost lasciviously at the cash. The younger figures to the right of Matthew, who is central to the seated group, are reminiscent of an earlier Caravaggio picture, the fortune-teller. Opposite them are Jesus and Peter. Jesus is pointing towards Matthew in a gesture of serene authority. It is here that the 'Creation of Adam' from the Sistine Chapel is being followed. The action and initiative are Christ's, which fact recalls for us the creator, but his arm is shaped in imitation of that of Adam. Christ is the Son of God incarnate, but also the second Adam, the perfect representative of the human race. Let us pause here. On the left we have activity as earthy as we can imagine – the greed of money-counters. These figures are seated, in a group of five, making a large horizontal composition. On the right we have Jesus and Peter, the representative of the Church, standing in vertical contradistinction to that composition. Jesus, the God man, joins the two groups, vertical and horizontal, by stretching forth his arm so that his hand reminds us of Adam even as the force of his decisive gesture testifies to his divinity. Matthew's reaction is deliberately exaggerated. He leans back and points to himself, saying 'Who, me?' As he does so, the light streaming into the room, which touches Christ's halo at a tangent, rests upon him.

This light illuminates not just the central character, but also the theological import of the picture. Earth (flat and horizontal) meets heaven (tall and vertical), and the two are linked by the arm of Jesus who embraces both heaven and earth in his one person, divine and human. When horizontal and vertical come together as they do here, what is the result? The answer, of course, is a cross. Caravaggio, as if not trusting us to make the connection, places that very crossover of up–down and side to side slap bang in our field of vision by framing a cross in the window that dominates the top of the picture.

The point should by now be too obvious to labour. This is a representation of the coming together of heaven and earth, of divine and human, and the consequences of that coming together are – quite simply – the cross. In the chapel – St Matthew's chapel – where this canvas hangs, on the opposite wall is a painting of the Saint's martyrdom, his stabbing, which the artist pointedly represents in a cruciform shape. The call to discipleship is a call to embrace the cross because to learn from Christ is to learn what it will mean for divinity to assume humanity. Human beings are created in the image of the God who pitches his tent among his people, the God who personifies love flowing into the hatred that meets it in the threatened security of human pride and power. The coming of Christ has turned upside down the preconceived notions of distance and safety from the all-consuming love of God: the call to follow, to trace those perpendicular lines until they meet in the crux of suffering and death, is the call to live the life of grace, a life that is cruciform because when creative love meets human self-concern, the cross of Christ is never far from view. To reflect the image of God we reflect the union of creator and redeemer, because the self-giving love of creation and redemption are one and the same.

All at once what Christ is

The *Call of St Matthew* shows us literally a cruciform image, but it invites us, more profoundly, to consider the contrasting aspects under which we can view the world and human beings within it. We can see the world of self only, or we can recognize that that world is only one part of a twofold reality. George Herbert's famous poem 'The Elixir' reminds us that we can look at glass and concentrate on it as glass, or look through it to see what lies beyond. The image of God in human beings is a cruciform image because it is the image of which Christ is the archetype. But it is also a cruciform image because it reveals to us the twofold aspect of every human being: a human with human limitations; a child of God with the infinite possibilities of grace.

Caravaggio is not for everyone, and so I suggest a return to the safe haven of poetry. Here are some famous lines by the Victorian Jesuit poet Gerard Manley Hopkins (1844–89):

As kingfishers catch fire, dragonflies draw flame;
    As tumbled over rim in roundy wells
    Stones ring; like each tucked string tells, each hung
    bell's
Bow swung finds tongue to fling out broad its name;
Each mortal thing does one thing and the same:
    Deals out that being indoors each one dwells;
    Selves – goes itself; myself it speaks and spells,
Crying What I do is me: for that I came.

I say more: the just man justices;
Keeps grace: that keeps all his goings graces;
    Acts in God's eye what in God's eye he is –
    Christ. For Christ plays in ten thousand places,
Lovely in limbs, and lovely in eyes not his
    To the Father through the features of men's faces.
    (Hopkins, *The Poems of Gerard Manley Hopkins*, p. 90)

This poem, perhaps Hopkins's most famous, contrasts the secular view of nature with the Christian view of creation:

> Each mortal thing does one thing and the same . . .;
> Selves – goes itself; myself it speaks and spells,
> Crying What I do is me, for that I came.

Rather than this individualistic world, Hopkins sees another:

> I say more: the just man justices;
> Keeps grace: that keeps all his goings graces;
>   Acts in God's eye what in God's eye he is –
>
>   Christ.

For Hopkins, as for Christian orthodoxy, creation and re-demption are not to be held apart. I am redeemed because, in the incarnation, death, resurrection and – importantly – the ascension of the Lord, Christ has become my humanity, Christ has transformed my nature so that when God looks on me in my sin, what he sees is Christ in his love.

St Irenaeus, writing at the end of the second century, says of Christ, 'He became what we are that we might became what he is' (Irenaeus, *Against Heresies* V). By identifying himself with human nature in the incarnation Christ has enabled all human beings to share in his true life, the divine life of heaven. This notion, set out by Paul in Romans 6, is the essence of Christian baptism: 'Do you not know that all of us who have been baptized into Christ have been baptized into his death?' (Romans 6.3). Paul goes on to say, 'If we have been united with him in a death like his, we will certainly be united with him in a resurrection like his,' (Romans 6.5), words that feature in the Easter Vigil service. The crucial phrase in the poem above must be, 'Acts in God's eye what in God's eye he is – Christ', for this is Hopkins's statement of Chrstian identity, the sharing in the life of God for which we were made in his image. That statement of identity is echoed strongly in the words of another remarkable example of Hopkins's poetic output.

The energy of particular things is for Hopkins a model for his idiosyncratic poetry, and a good example of that idiosyncrasy is the poem entitled 'That Nature is a Heraclitean Fire and the Comfort of the Resurrection'. The pre-Socratic philosopher Heraclitus held that all natural things are in a state of flux until they ultimately resolve into fire. This passing world is indeed a world that is passing, being generated and corrupted. Humanity falls into this fate as much as anything else, but if anything more bitterly, since pretensions of superiority and immortality bring us pathetically down to earth and end our grandiose claims not with a bang but with a whimper.

The very fact that this is a sonnet – a sonnet with 20 lines, no less – tells us something of its strangeness. The short, sharp monosyllables which tell of ordinary life trip through like water which drips rapidly away into nothing, like human life itself tramping relentlessly towards death:

> Mán, how fást his fíredint, his mark on mind, is gone!
> Bóth are in an únfáthomable, áll is in an enórmous dárk
> Drowned. O pity and indignation! Manshape, that shone
> Sheer off, disséveral, a stár, death blots black out; nor mark
> Is ány of him at áll so stárk
> But vastness blurs and time beats level. Enough! The Resurrection,
> A héart's-clarion! . . .

But with those words Hopkins turns away from the nihilism of pure nature to the resurrection hope that fires all creation. It is the resurrection that awaits the children of God at the sound of the last trumpet, so that the literally pathetic, even humorous collection of physical mess and moral weakness – 'the Jack, joke, poor potsherd, patch matchwood' – is in fact undying and indestructible, stronger, like diamond, than anything that assails it. Hopkins's brilliance with contrasts is on display. He uses the hardness of a k sound to make the long vowel of joke seem brittle and short next to jack, and even goes so far as to rhyme the words 'I am and' outrageously with 'diamond' – and in so doing poetically unites ragged humanity with its spiritual destiny.

> . . . Enough! The Resurrection,
> A héart's-clarion! Awáy grief's gásping, joyless days, dejection.
> Across my foundering deck shone
> A beacon, an eternal beam. Flesh fade, and mortal trash
> Fáll to the residuary worm; world's wildfire, leave but ash:
> In a flash, at a trumpet crash,
> I am all at once what Christ is, since he was what I am, and
> Thís Jack, jóke, poor pótsherd, patch, matchwood, immortal diamond,
> Is immortal diamond. (Hopkins, *The Poems of Gerard Manley Hopkins*, pp. 103–4)

Both these poems are poems offering a choice. We are invited to choose between two equally possible visions of human beings. The first is to see them as something purely

9

Grace and the sacramental life

By now it should be clear that grace is not an abstraction. The creative activity of God in pouring out the divine life is not an idea but the reality that supports and sustains the Christian life. There are many aspects of this life that we could identify as examples of grace in action. For some, talk of 'experience' in relation to God belongs only in the realm of the 'mystical', and so we might be inclined to think of some of the great teachers of the Christian spiritual tradition and the extraordinary lives of those figures whom the Church calls saints. But Christian experience is just the experience of living as a Christian, and since living is something practical done by material human beings, so Christian living is something practical that is done materially. Some of the principal material ways in which that living takes place are the acts of grace that we call 'sacraments'.

A sacrament is a sign of something holy. The word holy, or sacred, literally means 'set apart', and sacraments are physical actions in which both objects and people are, differently, set apart for God. The number of Christian sacraments has been disputed, but there is little disagreement about the central place of the two 'dominical sacraments' (sacraments 'of the Lord'), Baptism and the Eucharist, both of which feature significantly in the Gospels. Added to these two, most Christians would number Confirmation (in which the faith of a Christian is declared and 'confirmed'), Ordination (the making of deacons, priests and bishops), Reconciliation (the celebration of God's forgiveness through the individual confession of sins and the pronouncement of absolution), Unction – the anointing with oil of the sick and dying – and Marriage, or 'holy matrimony'.

According to Christian tradition, rooted as so often in the teaching of Augustine, a sacrament is a sacred sign that evokes a religious reality. Or, in another and common expression, it is a sign that 'effects that which it signifies'. What does this mean? It means first of all that sacraments are signs that are more than signs. If I follow the directions of a road sign, I am pointed a certain way in order to arrive at a particular end, but the end, the goal of my journey, is something altogether different from the sign that helped me navigate. A physical image that is used in a play may evoke a very powerful idea, but its relation to that idea remains that of an image. The fact that Macbeth's clothes fit him so badly after he has murdered King Duncan and succeeded to the throne is a sign that he is a usurper and has no place as sovereign. But the falsity of his position does not consist in the fact that his clothes don't fit, it consists in the fact that he is not the rightful king, but a killer.

Christianity teaches that Jesus of Nazareth is a sign of the reality of God. His words and actions signify the truth of God's all-embracing love, and his story points us in the direction of that truth. However, Jesus of Nazareth is also God himself incarnate. He is both a sign of the divine, and he is divinity personified. This paradox is the basis of the Christian sacramental life. Sacraments are actions that point to something beyond their visual and physical selves; and it is that something that God is bringing about through the celebration of the sacraments. Sacraments are, in that sense, vehicles of grace. They are real physical means by which God chooses to bring about the union with his own life that he offers in love to all people.

Grace poured out

Time for a note of caution. When we speak of the sacraments as 'vehicles of grace' we need to beware of the images we use. In Chapter 5 we noted the danger of our talk descending into 'hydraulics'. That word catches precisely the misunderstanding about grace that we have to clear up. Hydraulics, of course, is the study of the static and dynamic behaviour of fluids, and particularly applies to objects and mechanisms that are controlled by fluids. If we see grace as a fluid, something that sits static in a jug until it is poured out into us, then we will quickly develop a false understanding. We will be left with an understanding of grace as a commodity under our control. It becomes a resource or even a weapon, which we can use as we see fit. If we applied this misunderstanding to the celebration of the sacraments, then grace becomes something we can turn on or off with the recitation of some words. This looks a lot like most people's understanding of magic.

Fortunately for us these problems are not new. In the twelfth century, an interpreter of Augustine called Hugh of St Victor (named after an abbey in what is now Paris) wrote a treatise about the Christian sacraments and addressed this question. Hugh emphasized that sacraments are types of Christ himself, the source of all grace. Sacraments are gifts from God for the transmission of grace and the work of salvation, derived from Christ, the ultimate gift. The 'efficacy' of the sacraments, their ability to work as vehicles of grace, is not something that they contain in themselves. It is something that flowed only from the authority of Christ.

Despite these helpful clarifications, Hugh does use language that caused some later theologians a certain amount of caution. He compares the grace of God worked out in the sacraments to medicine that is contained within a vessel. More than a hundred years later, Thomas Aquinas has Hugh in mind when he affirms that the sacraments, in some sense, contain grace, but not as we may think. They are not simply a sign of grace, nor are they themselves properly a cause of grace. In themselves, sacraments contain grace as something incomplete, something that is transient. Sacramental activity is something always in motion, something that on its own is not enough. What worries Aquinas is the thought that we can turn the grace of God on and off the way we can turn on and off a water tap. Some might take this from Hugh's image of medicine in a bottle. Sacraments do contain grace, but a better analogy would be with water that is flowing through a pipe, in continuous motion. The source of that motion is Christ himself, the creative love of God personified. In other words, grace flows through the sacraments, because God is at work. Grace is not kept within the sacraments for us to help ourselves to as we choose, like children with cookies or Anglicans with gin.

This imagery helps us to avoid misunderstanding and misappropriating the grace of God. It also offers the basis of a properly cautious sacramental theology (something Hugh of St Victor was greatly concerned for, chastising those who seem to suggest that only via the sacraments can

God bring about the justification of any person). A sacrament brings about the reality to which it bears witness. So for example, the signs of food that Christians use in the Eucharist themselves effect the genuine spiritual nourishment, which is brought about by Christ in that sacrament. We are using the physical to celebrate the grace of God, to welcome and to accept God's initiative. In responding to God in this way, the Church acknowledges him as creator, and acknowledges his creation as good. Christians see in the physical stuff of God's world, the blessings and the benefits that he chooses in his love to shower on his children. By identifying particular things, and particular actions as sacramental, the Church has accepted a gift of God, a gift that helps believers to perceive and respond to God's love in action. Sacraments are, then, the celebration of creation, that bringing of something out of nothing that gives us the physical and material context in which all life is lived.

None of this is about fluid dynamics. The grace of God, the self-giving love of Father, Son and Holy Spirit, is always at work and always being given. We should remind ourselves here of the 'cruciform' image or 'twofold aspect' which has been emphasized throughout this book. We can, if we so wish, see the activities of Christian life and worship as thoroughly worldly things. We can concentrate, in other words, on the 'things' of sacramental life – the pouring of water, the breaking of bread – rather than the sacraments themselves. It is just such an error that the earlier theologians mentioned above were concerned to avoid because if we do concentrate on the material – as if the sacraments were something under our control, not the activity of Christ – we are talking only in worldly terms. The 'healing', to use Hugh's imagery, that the sacraments can bring about could thus only be a worldly healing. It would be a sort of making us feel better, and would remind us of those interpretations of Christianity (and other religious practice) that suggest that religion is there to make us feel good. If we are talking about grace, however, we are talking about being united with the life of God. We need to combine our worldly talk with talk of the divine. Christian discussion of the sacraments is always twofold because sacraments are material things, but also much more than material things. As we saw in the previous chapter, the same is true of human beings. And, in both cases, it is true because the same is true of Jesus Christ.

Life on board the ark

In the Gospel of Mark we find two stories (both paralleled in Matthew's Gospel) in which Jesus exercises authority over the elements in order to save his disciples from shipwreck and drowning. The second of these stories, in Mark 6, has the disciples heading across to the other side of the lake on their own, while Jesus takes time to pray. Standing alone on the land, he sees the boat and its inhabitants struggling against the wind, and walks out to them across the water. They cry out in fear, assuming him to be a ghost, but he reassures them with the words 'It is I' – the words *ego eimi* in Greek, the same divine utterance as was heard by Moses when he encountered Yahweh, the God of Israel, in the burning bush (Exodus 3). As Jesus gets into the boat the wind drops, and the disciples are both rescued and astounded. The earlier story is slightly different. In it, Jesus is in the boat throughout the journey. He is asleep as the storm rises, as was another biblical passenger – the fleeing prophet Jonah who thinks he can escape the presence of the God who made the heavens and the earth by taking a long boat trip. Jesus, according to Mark, does not escape that presence, he provides it. In the book of Jonah, the storm abates when the terrified sailors cast the prophet out of the boat, distancing themselves from the disobedient fugitive who attracts such dramatic divine attention. In the Gospel of Mark, the storm drops when Jesus tells it to drop. He is woken by his panicking companions and restores calm with a couple of words.

Throughout Christian history the image of a ship on which we travel has been a popular biblical source for reflection on the life of the Church – be it the Ark of Noah and his family, or the smaller crafts of the Galilean disciples. Modern scholars have interpreted both of these miracle stories as alluding to the struggles of the early Christian communities. To those living in the face of rejection or persecution, they give an assurance of the saving presence of Jesus. The story of walking on the water we might take as an image of the grace God pours into his Church to save and sustain it. But the earlier story is perhaps a better starting point, because there is no point in the proceedings at which Jesus is not present. The Church should not be understood as something that carries on on its own, and every so often needs inspiration – the breathing in of the Spirit – or a miraculous deliverance from a God who was not there to begin with. The Church exists because God creates and sustains it, and the Church is the locus of the life of grace because God chooses people, things and relationships through which to work.

If we consider the Church along the same lines as our consideration of grace and its action, we will see that we could try to understand the Christian community as the vehicle of grace in the same way as we might understand a static jug to contain grace. If that is our model, then the Church is at human disposal, and is not the Body of Christ. If, however, we think of the Church not as something that contains so much as something that receives, we would do better. We will be able to continue to articulate our notion of grace as the love of God in action, not in abstract. The corporate life of Christians is not defined by their common belief or practice. It is defined by their being 'in Christ' – their baptism into the life, death and resurrection of the Son of God incarnate, the source of all grace. As we have seen, being 'in Christ' is not something that is achieved, a point that we reach so that we can then relax. Being 'in Christ' means being united to the dynamic life of the Trinity, to the eternal motion of self-giving love that is Father, Son and Holy Spirit.

A vessel such as a ship can be a poor image of the Church if we think of the Church as something separatist or ghettoized, defined against the world in a straightforward contrast of good and bad. When discussing Augustine and Pelagius, we saw that attempts to oppose the grace of God to human life, as if divine and human agency were opposites within the same framework, were doomed to give a distorting picture. Likewise, an understanding of a perfect Church in complete contradistinction to everything outside it is an understanding of a Church that needs only to give, and has nothing to receive. The life of discipleship that we stressed in Chapter 7 is, however, a pilgrim life. The Christian Church is in fact defined by the Holy Spirit – it receives its life and existence only because it is a community seeking to be led by the Spirit into ever closer union with God. As with the sacraments, the only basis and authority for this life can be that of Christ himself.

The Church exists because human beings are not as good at responding to the love of God as they could be. Their divine potential, the image of God within them, is not something to which they always attain. Acting as individuals to try to discern the will of God and follow where the Spirit leads is difficult. Coming together with one's fellow Christians and acknowledging the struggle to which the life of grace calls us (we are reminded again of Bonhoeffer) is an act of humility, itself a Christian virtue. We do not have all the answers. And we are part of something that is far larger than here and now and me and mine. We are part of the Body of Christ.

The identity of the Christian life

For Paul, we are in Christ because we have been baptized into his death and resurrection. Baptism, as we saw in Chapter 2, is an act of unity with the life of God. It joins our lives to the life and death of Jesus so that we are united with him in his crucifixion and his rising to new life. The gospel narratives begin their account of the adult Jesus' ministry by reporting his being baptized by John the Baptist. (The Fourth Gospel presupposes but does not actually contain the event.) The evangelists, knowing that Jesus had been baptized by John, struggle with the idea. They are afraid that it suggests John's superiority, and we see this in their transmission of the story. Jesus comes to John to be baptized, but because this action confuses a Christian sense of the order of things, we hear John himself ask the question: 'I need to be baptized by you, and do you come to me?' It should be the other way round. But Jesus persists: 'Let it be so for now; for it is proper for us in this way to fulfil all righteousness' (Matthew 3.14–15).

Jesus' coming to John is an affirmation of John's ministry of baptism, but it is also a transformation of that ministry. Before Jesus' appearance, John has been a forerunner, a prophetic voice preparing his hearers for something, or rather someone, who will turn the world upside down. Readying them for this decisive moment, he calls them to repentance by baptism – they are to be changed, to turn away from sin to focus on the coming Kingdom of God. However, as soon as Jesus appears in person, John's ministry is transformed. He is now not a forerunner, but a witness. He is marked out in the Fourth Gospel as the one who proclaims Jesus' true identity: Look, he exhorts his listeners, this is the lamb of God, who takes away the sin of the world. The identity of John the Baptist, his part in God's plan of redemption, is changed by the presence of Jesus and by the act of his baptism. John's previous ministry is commended, and a new ministry is inaugurated.

This first action of the adult Jesus – the act of being baptized – is in fact something passive: Jesus is undergoing an action that somebody else performs. In obedience to the will of his father, and in affirmation of the baptismal ministry of John, he is the recipient of something, something human and something divine, the action of John and the action of the Father. This passivity is a clue to our understanding of the grace at work in baptism. By offering himself to the world and to the Father in baptism, he is prefiguring the offering of his whole life, which his ministry and message will demand. Just as that offering of perfect life on the cross of this world transforms the very human sin to which it is surrendered, so in the baptism of Christ, the Word made flesh is offered to the waters of the Jordan in order to transform all waters, all worlds. In being baptized, Jesus is in fact baptizing the world himself. His identity as divine and human means that he is both the recipient and the agent of baptism. Jesus of Nazareth is blessed by the water, but Jesus Christ blesses the waters of the Jordan and the waters of the whole earth. They are to be set apart for God's purposes, to be used for the baptism of every Christian. The world is being taken by God to be used afresh for his purposes. So, again, we have a twofold aspect to consider. Jesus both commends the ministry of John and transforms it; Jesus both submits of the waters of baptism, and consecrates them. What God has made is good. What God has remade in Christ is better.

Baptism both affirms and transforms human identity. All human beings are the beloved children of God created in his image. In an entirely straightforward and mundane sense (the word is chosen carefully) a human being is the same person after being baptized as before. But paradoxically, and – which is more important – sacramentally, that human being is also a different person. By calling people to baptism God has affirmed his love for humans as they are; and by the anointing of his life-giving Spirit he has made them into something new. God has transformed our identity not in discontinuity with what has gone before, but by adding to our human life the divine life of Christ, to which we are united in baptism.

The story of the baptism of Christ is a Trinitarian story: the Son submits to baptism; the Father is heard to declare his identity; the Spirit is seen as the source of that new life. The letter to the Hebrews speaks of the Son reflecting the image of God and bearing 'the exact imprint of God's very being' (Hebrews 1.3). Being united with Christ in baptism is sharing that identity, being adopted as God's children by grace, no longer a slave but a son, as Galatians has it. The Greek word for stamp, used in Hebrews, is the word 'character', and that word has a significant influence in Christian teaching on the sacramental life of grace. In the fifth century, a great Christian teacher wrote in the guise of an incidental New Testament figure, a man called Dionysius the Areopagite, who is described in Acts 17 as one who joined Paul and believed after hearing the Apostle preach in Athens. This theologian, whom we now call 'Pseudo-Dionysius', suggested that the sacramental life of the Church imparts the character, the stamp of identity, that the believer requires to be admitted to the worshipping community that reaches to heaven.

Ordering grace

As with all the effects of grace, this sacramental character is the gift of Christ himself, a confirmation of the baptismal identity given to all who are 'in Christ'. One particular, and sometimes controversial, aspect of sacramental character is the result of one particular sacrament: the sacrament of orders. Some human beings are set apart by God to be, and to function as, peculiar kinds of Christian ministers. These we call bishops, priests and deacons: they are the recipients of 'ordination'.

When we think of Holy Orders, and especially when we think of priesthood, the misunderstandings of grace against which we have been guarding are apt to resurface. A priest can be thought of as one who possesses grace and who has the power to use it or not use it as wished. Our understanding of the dynamic nature of grace in and through the sacraments, and this movement being the basis for a doctrine of a pilgrim Church led in the Spirit, ought to preclude such a caricature. But the 'problem' of ordination remains. Why should God work in this way?

The answer to such questions should always be agnosticism – Christian theology is not an attempt to explain the will of God, it is an attempt to reflect upon the encounter with God in Jesus Christ. That encounter takes many forms in many contexts, but the community of the Church is essential among them, simply because the New Testament witnesses to that context. The story of Christianity is the story of God working in and through people – recreating the world in Christ, and giving the new life Christ brings about to all the baptized. Some of those who are baptized are called to minister as bishops, priests and deacons. Most are not. But there is nothing special about those who are called to mark them out from the rest of the baptized – as we saw in Chapter 6, God's will should not be imagined as the arbitrary whim of capricious power. All who are baptized share in the life of Christ and all could receive the grace of orders. Baptism is what gives us Christian identity: for some, ordination follows, but it can only follow because the grace of God has united us to Christ already as baptized members of the Church. (This theology of baptism is the reason why we cannot theologically exclude people from those who might be called to be ordained simply on grounds of gender.)

Ordination has its roots in the Gospels. Jesus has many followers, and some of those followers are chosen for particular ministries. The apostles are marked out and named, the Twelve who represent the new Israel of God. Elsewhere in the New Testament we read of them praying and laying hands on others in order to commission and inspire them to further the ministry of the gospel. Writing to the Corinthians, Paul reminds his readers that the community should be seen as a body with many parts – apostles, prophets, teachers, miracle workers, healers, helpers, administrators and so on. Those whom the Church would go on to describe as ordained – the threefold orders of bishop, priest and deacon, orders that we glimpse in the New Testament but emerge fully only later – are particular examples among many possibilities of Christian ministry, and all who are used by God can rightly be described as vehicles of God's grace.

Some sacraments, however, are celebrated only with the participation of priests or bishops. This is so because ordination itself is a sacrament, it imparts a particular character – the result of grace – so that a particular person can exist in a particular way. It means that someone can be something, not simply do something. A priest is no different from any other person except that he or she is ordained. But this is a big 'except'. It cannot be explained by a series of descriptive terms, as can the difference between a virtuoso violinist and an international goalkeeper. Physical or personal characteristics are something entirely different from sacramental character. Just as we can articulate – speak words about – the redemptive love of God without being able to explain it, so the sacramental act of grace that makes baptized people baptized, or ordained people ordained, is not something for which we can provide a formulaic or explanatory account.

The British philosopher Sir Peter Strawson wrote a celebrated book about the problem of 'personal identity' – why is a person correctly called a person and not simply a bundle of cells? and similar questions. In it he argued that we simply have to accept the word 'person' as 'logically primitive'. It does not allow a smaller division into atomic parts, which we can add together to make 'a person'. We start from knowing how to use that word, and proceed from that point. I think we should make the same sort of move when speaking of the action of God in the sacramental life. What makes a baptized person 'baptized' is the grace of God. The difference between an ordained person and one who is not ordained is – simply but not trivially – that one of them is ordained and the other is not. In one case, God has acted in a particular way that we cannot explain, and in another case he has not (though he has doubtless acted in all sorts of particular ways in relation to that person, as everyone else). In the case of a priest, the cruciform nature of grace has been worked out so that a baptized person both is the same as every other Christian – he or she is a baptized person – and is not – because he or she is a priest.

A priest is the recipient of grace, and so priesthood – like all the sacraments – has its basis in Christ. We saw in Chapter 4 that the life of Christ with which Christians are united by grace is the life of self-giving love. A priest lives out this life of self-giving, of offering, in a particular way. To offer something to God is what it means to be a priest, and the heart of all Christian offering is the real offering of Christ himself in the crown of the Church's sacramental life, the celebration of the Eucharist.

Offering everything

Almost everything that has been said about grace will, I hope, be repeated in an account of the Eucharist. This central Christian action is the Church's living out of God's salvation. It is the celebration of Gods initiative in drawing our life into union with his. The Eucharist makes the Church, because it is the body of Christ by which the Body of Christ must live. Long before modern dietary concerns were all the rage, the Christian Church had maintained that we are what we eat.

As we have said, the theology of grace is a theology of action, and the action of God is not something located in the past. No reader of the Gospels could easily conclude that those who wrote them did so to ossify or freeze the ministry of Jesus; the gospel narratives come to us as the actions of a drama, and it is a drama that each Christian is always living out. Earlier we looked at the story of the stilling of the storm. Its use as an image of Christ's care for his Church is a straightforward example of this. There are many Christian actions – the actions of worship and prayer, the actions of love and generosity – to which Christians are called. However, as we have repeatedly maintained when discussing grace and the sacraments, the root of Christian action has to be Christ himself; if Christ is not present in his Church, in the midst of his people's drama as director and as principal artist, then the actions of Christian people – however charitable – will be their actions, not Christ's.

So at the centre of the Christian life there should be and is a focus on the presence of Christ among his people, and this is nowhere clearer than in the drama of the Eucharist, because the Eucharist is the whole Christian story acted out in miniature. The offering of the sinless Son of God for sinful women and men is not a past event. The fact that the crucifixion is a historical event long past in the human scheme of things is not something that restricts our understanding of God's eternal act. The divine is not restricted by change and time as people are. The incarnate humanity of Christ, offered, sacrificed, risen and ascended, is always part of the Godhead. It is real humanity drawn up into God and eternally representing humanity to God. This is not representation in our ordinary sense of the word – depicting, or being an image for. It is re-presenting, offering something again. The perfect human life lived out in Christ is offered in its perfection so that all human imperfections are overlooked.

In the Eucharist, bread and wine – simple, physical gifts – are brought and offered to God: the simple stuff of life offered to its author. God receives those gifts, takes them, transforms them and then offers them back to the Church, whose offering he transforms. That is the miracle of the Eucharist – by grace people offer, and God transforms so as to unite human offering with the perfect offering of the Son to the Father. Those who receive communion seem only to receive what was first offered – the signs of bread and wine – but in reality they receive the gift of God himself. God gives himself in this sacrament so that human beings are drawn up into the worship of heaven. In this worship it is the humanity of Christ that plays our part, ensuring that when God looks towards his human children what he sees is Christ. Rather than our selfishness, he sees the self-giving love of the perfect Son. The Victorian theologian and hymn writer William Bright put it beautifully: 'Look, Father, look on his anointed face, And only look on us as found in him' (*New English Hymnal*, no. 273). Bright was no Gerard Manley Hopkins, but both knew that in Christ humanity finds its perfect image. This image is the gift of grace to those who are baptized into Christ's body and sustained by the presence of his risen life.

The penultimate supper

In 1976, a theatrical performance entitled *A Poke in the Eye with a Sharp Stick* became the first in a series of benefit shows by comedians performed in aid of Amnesty

International. One sketch first performed in this show, by John Cleese and Jonathan Lynn, has become known as 'the penultimate supper'. In it, Michelangelo is upbraided by the Pope for producing a rather outlandish painting of Our Lord's final meal on this earth. The pontifical gripes include the fact that the picture shows twenty-eight disciples and three Christs. The artist, rather pleased by his well-filled canvas, is firmly told that there were twelve disciples present, one Christ, and no waiters, cabaret or friends. Michelangelo's solution is to change not the painting, but its title. 'I've got it! We'll call it the Penultimate Supper . . . . there must've been one. I mean, if there was a last one, there must have been one before that, right?' (Cleese, *The Golden Skits*, 1984, p. 39).

Admirers of the Monty Python team (who wrote this sketch and included it in their 1982 revue *Live at the Hollywood Bowl*) have observed a close parallel with events in the life of the great sixteenth-century painter Veronese. His 1573 canvas, *The Supper at the House of Levi*, was originally intended as a picture of the Last Supper but had its title changed as a result of objections from the Holy Office (or Inquisition). The church authorities felt that the representation of many characters other than the twelve disciples (the transcript of the hearing mentions 'buffoon, drunken Germans, dwarfs and other such absurdities' Rearick, *The Art of Paolo Veronese 1528–1588*, p. 104) was impious and inappropriate. The painting's new title and original intention are sometimes combined by referring to it as 'The Last Supper at the House of Levi', the implication presumably being that, since we know from the Gospels that Jesus had supper at the house of Levi, there must have been a last time that this happened.

The irony is heavy, but as we conclude our examination of the Christian doctrine of grace, we might observe that each celebration of the Eucharist is, in a sense, 'the penultimate supper'. Every Eucharistic celebration is both the sign and the reality of the all-embracing love of God. The Eucharist is the gift of grace that flows from Christ at the centre and touches all human life, just as the remarkable canvas now hanging in Venice displays such energy, vitality and variety, the very things that alarmed the artist's contemporaries. Every Eucharist is 'the penultimate supper' because every Eucharist anticipates the fellowship with Christ that characterizes the Kingdom of God.

Of course every Eucharist is also the Last Supper, in that it re-enacts the events of Jesus' passion and constitutes the feast by which all members of the Church are joined, as disciples, in fellowship with the Son of God who offers himself for them. But each earthly Eucharist is also something heavenly, an anticipation of the Kingdom that will be finally revealed in the messianic banquet, the marriage supper of the Lamb of God that we read of in the book of Revelation. The 'ultimate supper', in this sense, is the stuff of the end time. It is *the* gathering in of all nations, peoples and worlds, the final feast of heaven to which all are invited by grace. And every single Eucharist – every celebration in which by grace we truly participate in the offering of the Son to the Father and truly are nourished by the body of Christ – is as close to that final feast as earthly life will allow. Every Eucharist is the 'penultimate supper', the fellowship with Christ that can only be bettered by the truly blessed vision enjoyed by those united to the life of the Trinity.

That unity is the gift of grace. The life of grace, the sacramental life of every Christian, is the fullest and richest

Select bibliography

Anselm of Canterbury, ed. Brian Davies and G. R. Evans, 1998, *The Major Works*, Oxford: Oxford University Press.

Aquinas, Thomas, 1963–1975 *Summa Theologiae*, 60 vols, Cambridge: Cambridge University Press.

Augustine of Hippo, tr. Henry Chadwick, 1991, *Confessions*, Oxford: Oxford University Press.

Augustine of Hippo, tr. Thomas Williams, 1993, *On Free Choice of the Will*, Indianapolis: Hackett.

Augustine of Hippo, ed. Philip Schaff, 2007, *Anti-Pelagian Writings,* Nicene and Post-Nicene Fathers, First Series, vol. 5, New York: Cosimo.

Augustine of Hippo, ed. Philip Schaff, 2007, *Gospel of John, First Epistle of John,* Soliloquies, tr. John Gibb, Nicene and Post Nicene Fathers, First Series, vol. 7, New York: Cosimo.

Karl Barth, ed. G. W. Bromiley and T. F. Torrance, 1936–77, *Church Dogmatics,* 13 vols, Edinburgh: T & T Clark.

Dietrich Bonhoeffer, ed. Eberhard Bethge, 1971, *Letters and Papers from Prison*, London: SCM Press.

Dietrich Bonhoeffer, tr. Barbara Green and Reinhard Krauss, 2003, *Discipleship*, Minneapolis: Fortress Press.

Gerald Bonner, 2007, *Freedom and Necessity: St Augustine's Teaching on Divine Power and Human Freedom*, Washington DC: Catholic University of America Press.

John Calvin, ed. John T. McNeill, 1960, *Institutes of the Christian Religion*, 2 vols, The Library of Christian Classics 20–21, Philadelphia: Westminster, 1960.

John Cleese, 1984, *The Golden Skits of Muriel Volestrangler FRHS and Bar*, London: Methuen.

The Cloud of Unknowing, tr. and ed. James Walsh, 1981, Mahwah NJ: Paulist Press.

Brian Davies, 1992, *The Thought of Thomas Aquinas*, Oxford: Oxford University Press.

John Donne, ed. John Carey, 1990, *John Donne: A Critical Edition of the Major Works*, Oxford: Oxford University Press.

Philip Endean, 2001, *Karl Rahner and Ignatian Spirituality*, Oxford: Oxford University Press.

Alastair Fowler (ed.), 1991, *The New Oxford Book of Seventeenth-Century Verse*, Oxford: Oxford University Press.

Roger Haight, 1979, *The Experience and Language of Grace*, Mahwah NJ: Paulist Press.

George Herbert, ed. John Tobin, 1991, *The Complete English Poems*, London: Penguin.

Gerard Manley Hopkins, ed. W. H. Gardner and N. H. MacKenzie, 1970[1967], *The Poems of Gerard Manley Hopkins*, Oxford: Oxford University Press.

Hymns and Psalms: A Methodist and Ecumenical Hymnbook, 1983, London: Methodist Publishing House.

Irenaeus of Lyons, *Against Heresies*, ed. Alexander Roberts, James Donaldson and Arthur Cleveland Coxe, 2007[1884], *The Ante-Nicene Fathers Volume I*, New York: Cosimo.

Julian of Norwich, tr. Edmund College and James Walsh, 1978, *Showings*, Mahwah NJ: Paulist Press.

Terrance W. Klein, 2007, *Wittgenstein and the Metaphysics of Grace*, Oxford: Oxford University Press.

Henri de Lubac, 1946, *Surnaturel: études historique*, Paris: Aubier.

Herbert McCabe, 2008, *On Aquinas*, London: Continuum.

Herbert McCabe, 1987, *God Matters*, London: Geoffrey Chapman.

John Milbank, 2003, *Being Reconciled: Ontology and Pardon*, London: Routledge.

John Milbank, 2005, *The Suspended Middle: Henri de Lubac and the Debate Concerning the Supernatural*, London: SCM Press.

New English Hymnal, 1986, Norwich: Canterbury Press.

Karl Rahner, 1961–92, *Theological Investigations*, 23 vols, London: Darton, Longman and Todd.

Karl Rahner, tr. William V. Dych, 1968, *Spirit in the World*, London: Sheed and Ward.

BIBLIOGRAPHY

W. R. Rearick, 1988, *The Art of Paolo Veronese 1528–1588*, Washington DC: National Gallery of Art.

E. P. Sanders, 1977, *Paul and Palestinian Judaism*, London: SCM Press.

E. P. Sanders, 2001, *Paul: A Very Short Introduction*, Oxford: Oxford University Press.

Stephen Sondheim, 2010, *Finishing the Hat: Collected Lyrics (1954–1981)*, New York: Random House.

P. F. Strawson, 1959, *Individuals: an essay in descriptive metaphysics*, London: Routledge.

Tertullian, tr. T. R. Glover, 1966, *Apology*, Loeb Classical Library, Cambridge MA: Harvard University Press.

Rowan Williams, 1979, *The Wound of Knowledge*, London: Darton, Longman and Todd.

Rowan Williams, 2000, *On Christian Theology*, Oxford: Blackwell.

Ludwig Wittgenstein, tr. G. E. M. Anscombe, 1967, *Philosophical Investigations*, Oxford: Blackwell.

Index